Applied Faith: 101

Understanding The Origin, Principles And Dimensions Of Your Christian Faith

Melvin E. Barnett

Copyright © 2011 Gateswood Press / Melvin E. Barnett

All rights reserved. No part of this book may be used or reproduced in any manner whatsoever without written permission except for reprints in the context of reviews.

www.melvinbarnett.com

ISBN: 978-0615550664

Printed In The United States of America

Dedication

This book is dedicated in memory of Reverend James Walter Rutland, Jr. Brother Walter was a friend, Elder, and fellow Pastor who was faithful to his family and friends; but more than anything he was faithful to his Lord.

November 20, 1940 – September 13, 2011

Contents

	Acknowledgments	i
1	Now Faith Is…	1
2	The Journey Ahead	7
3	Outside Of God's Grace	15
4	Man's Created Purpose	25
5	Man's Duties in the Garden	33
6	Who Is In Control Of The Earth?	53
7	The Effects Of Man's Sin In The Garden	61
8	The Initial Will Of God For Man	75
9	A Change Of Plans	95
10	Why Hast Thou Forsaken Me?	101
11	Forsaken In Your Own Hometown	113
12	God Wants Your Present, Not Your Past	119
13	DNA and Faith	123
14	God Never Changes, People Do	131
15	The Spirit Of Fear	145
16	Faith Fosters Fortune	157
17	The Plan Of Salvation	169
	About the Author	175

Acknowledgements

Most importantly, I would like to thank those who have prayed and supported this ministry over the past years. Thanks to my wife, family, and close friends who have been a personal encouragement throughout years of ministry.

Thanks to my Editor, Rhetta J. Goodman, for her patience, talents, and long time friendship.

1 | Now Faith Is

Now faith is the substance of things hoped for, the evidence of things not seen. (Hebrews 11:1-1 KJV)

Before understanding how to apply faith one must completely understand what faith is and moreover what it isn't. The above passage defines faith in a nutshell. To be very candid, there is a neither better nor a more concise definition of faith found anywhere else. For thousands of years people have been trying to understand faith and define it in their own terms, but you and I must accept what the Word of God says about faith.

Visual matter isn't faith. What you can see, touch, hear, smell and taste is not faith at all; those things are called reality. In our present earthly existence our senses protect us, fulfill us, excite us, warn us, but they only work in our mortal dimension; this present mortal dimension is what you and I call reality. Faith goes beyond reality and exists in a whole different dimension. Faith and reality cannot exist on the same side of a coin; unfortunately, this truth hinders many people from truly understanding faith. Why the hindrance? Because man lives and functions in a world of realities, or at least what they perceive as real. After all, seeing is believing!

However, faith is VERY real, it just exists in a whole other dimension than the one that the natural man abides in. Faith is an essential part of our relationship with God. Every aspect of our relationship with God is built on some degree of Faith. Your intimacy with God is determined by your faith. In simple terms, everything that has anything to do with man and his relationship with God is built on faith, not reality.

Chapter 1: Now Faith Is

Faith is the very substance and distance between man and God. It is very difficult in letting go of our senses and trusting what some may call "thin air." You and I are not programmed to just openly trust without some process of verification. Trust is an issue that many of us have had to deal with and often those dealings have created a lot of pain. I wish I could be more optimistic in defining Faith, but I can't. I would be fraudulent to try and bring any sense of reality to Faith. Anyone else that would attempt to rationalize Faith into an object that can be sensed by our human body is simply being deceitful or at least misguided in their efforts.

Our Salvation begins in reaching out by Faith to claim hold to Grace (God's unmerited favor). Yes, it is literally thin air between our reality and God's Grace. However, the transformation is real and even though it is by faith it WILL produce real changes that can be noticed in an individual. The reality of our transformation is crystal clear as the Bible says, " *Therefore if any man be in Christ, he is a new creature: old things are passed away; behold, all things are become new (2 Corinthians 5:17)."* From the inception of this "new creature" everything in our life as it pertains to God in any way is by faith from the moment of transformation.

If you continue in Hebrews 11, you will see in verse 2, *"For by it the elders obtained a good report"*. By what? Faith. Once again, all that we will ever obtain from God will be by faith. If we excel in our Christian walk it will be by Faith alone. If we become stagnant in our walk with the Lord it will be because we have backslidden or, we have failed to exercise our faith, which some would argue are one in the same.

It is by faith we have spiritual sight. What is a reality to God that has not manifested before our eyes is obtained and held onto by faith. For instance, we have not seen the second coming of our Lord; however, we believe it to be true as if it has happened in the natural. Verse 3 continues, "Through faith we understand that the worlds were framed by the word of God, so that things which are seen were not made of things which do appear." You and I didn't see the worlds framed together, yet we surely accept it to be historical fact. We believe that God parted the Red Sea just as if we were there watching as Moses led the Children of Israel across. We believe that Jesus hung on the Cross and bore the sins of the world for all mankind to ultimately accept unto Salvation. As real as these facts are to us, they are received by faith.

As believers, it is our unwavering faith that pleases God. We receive the Word of God by Faith. We hold dear to the great doctrines of the Bible by faith. We live a consecrated life because of our Faith in God. Every aspect of our life should reflect our faith. Where we live, where we work, who our friends are, where we spend our time, who and how we love, all these dimensions of our life are to be rooted in our faith. You see God wants to literally inundate every inch of our body, soul and spirit through the work of the Holy Spirit living inside of us. Our faith will determine just how much of our lives we are willing to turn over to him. Total trust is what God wants from each of us. Fact is, if we are ever going to please God we must learn to live by faith each and every day. The bible declares that without faith it is impossible for us to please God.

> *But without faith it is impossible to please him: for he that cometh to God must believe that he is, and that he is a rewarder of them that diligently seek him. (Hebrews 11:6)*

A life of faith is a life of action. As Christians we can't just claim faith without manifesting some action. Where there is faith, there will be evidence of action; the Bible refers to these actions as "works." Consider the scriptures below:

> *What doth it profit, my brethren, though a man say he hath faith, and have not works? can faith save him? [15] If a brother or sister be naked, and destitute of daily food, [16] And one of you say unto them, Depart in peace, be ye warmed and filled; notwithstanding ye give them not those things which are needful to the body; what doth it profit? [17] Even so faith, if it hath not works, is dead, being alone. [18] Yea, a man may say, Thou hast faith, and I have works: shew me thy faith without thy works, and I will shew thee my faith by my works. [19] Thou believest that there is one God; thou doest well: the devils also believe, and tremble. [20] But wilt thou know, O vain man, that faith without works is dead? (James 2:14-20)*

Faith in action secures the immediate need. Faith without "works" has no profit to the world. Our prayers and sympathy for the calamities of this world have their place, but without action we bring no substance to the table. Faith in action is manifested by people in action, groups in action and certainly a church in action. No action is a clear sign of absent faith or at least, the lack thereof. Our passage declares that *"the devils also believe and tremble,"* yet belief, or faith, is of no value without works. Believing isn't enough. Actions are necessary to produce faith, and faith will always produce works.

Chapter 1: Now Faith Is

Faith is very discriminating. You and I will live the rest of our lives choosing faith over what is naturally concrete. Shall we believe God or trust in what we naturally see, hear, feel, smell and taste? You and I must stay focused on what is reality. Is reality that we can receive through our five senses? No. All that we sense is temporary although it is real to us in the dimension we currently live. What we cannot sense in the natural is actually real and moreover, eternal.

> *While we look not at the things which are seen, but at the things which are not seen: for the things which are seen are temporal; but the things which are not seen are eternal. (2 Corinthians 4:18)*

As stated, we as Christians will spend the rest of our lives on earth living by faith. It is a concept that is alien to this world. Non-Christians will never understand the things that pertain to your faith. Sadly they honestly haven't the capacity to comprehend spiritual matters. Their understanding and articulation of things spiritual will be absolutely secular in nature. Most likely you will have friends and loved ones that will earnestly try and steer you in a direction that seems only sensible to them. Perhaps many of them will honestly have your best interests in mind as they seek to influence you; however, without the presence of the Holy Spirit living in them they will discern the matters of the spirit through a secular prism. Consider the scripture below:

> *But the natural man receiveth not the things of the Spirit of God: for they are foolishness unto him: neither can he know them, because they are spiritually discerned. (1 Corinthians 2:14)*

The natural man holds to what is tangible. The spirit man will cling to what is spiritual. Sadly, in each of us is a continual war against what is both natural and spiritual. The battles are unending, but the Lord helps us by giving us strength to overcome the natural man by discerning spiritual matters. Even as Christians, there is a constant battle raging between the natural (carnal) man which is flesh and the spirit man. The natural man has no regard for sin. The flesh openly defies any measure of faith. In the scripture below we see Paul in a battle of carnality and spirit.

> *For we know that the law is spiritual: but I am carnal, sold under sin.* [15] *For that which I do I allow not: for what I would, that do I not; but what I hate, that do I.* [16] *If then I do that which I would not, I consent unto the law that it is good.* [17] *Now then it is no more I that do it, but sin that dwelleth in me.* [18] *For I know that in me (that is, in my flesh,) dwelleth*

> *no good thing: for to will is present with me; but how to perform that which is good I find not. [19] For the good that I would I do not: but the evil which I would not, that I do. [20] Now if I do that I would not, it is no more I that do it, but sin that dwelleth in me. (Romans 7:14-20)*

Our faith will determine how we resolve matters in this current dimension of reality. We must apply Faith at every turn in life. No matter the issues at hand, our faith must play a constant role in our decisions. We must stand firm and never turn back. We must lift up a banner of faith and proceed through every trial that comes our way. Every calamity that strikes around us must be met with hostile force, a force that puts our faith on the offensive. Every mountain you move will be moved by faith. Our faith must be sure, constant and progressive.

> *Let us hold fast the profession of our faith without wavering; (for he is faithful that promised;) (Hebrews 10:23)*

Beloved, we must resolve to move beyond the dimension of this life and take hold of our faith in God. We cannot attempt living in two worlds that are at polar opposites with one another. The headache and pure hardship of indecisive living between a lifestyle of faith or a mortal approach to life will lead to spiritual burnout and despair. Remember that which is visible is temporal and that which is invisible to the natural man is eternal. The only way to live by faith is to walk by faith. The Bible says, *"For we walk by faith, not by sight (2 Corinthians 5:7):"*

As we move on from here we will explore the deep truths of faith. We will see the existence of faith in every aspect of life from the creation of man in the Garden, to holding down a forty hour job that challenges us each and every day. We will explore the effects of sin and how it shaped the world. We will see God's will for each of us and the absolute necessity to approach living each day by faith. We will understand rejection, fear and abandonment through the prism of faith. Come with me as we journey ahead.

2 | The Journey Ahead

The journey ahead gives you a little insight into my life, the ups and downs and the struggles that lead to writing this book. This chapter is a brief summary of ministry as I lived it from my early twenties to present day.

Since the day I typed the first words to this book (1995), much water has passed under the bridge. I started writing when I was single and not looking for a wife. There was a time when I was married to the church – so to speak. That era (mindset) didn't last as long as I thought it would. Today, I am a happily married man with wonderful children. The Lord has been so good to me in so many ways. He has answered so many prayers. The Lord has led me down wonderful roads filled with joy and great adventure.

The adventure has been exciting, but the road has often been long, cold, rough, and at times very lonely. There have been times I have cried myself to sleep in desperation before the Lord, and, it seemed He wasn't even present. Some of the longest, toughest nights were those spent in the earlier hours, shaking hands, hugging necks, conversing and laughing in rooms filled with great joy, only later to find myself driving alone down a long, winding country road leading to my house, as well as to the end to a long day and often longer night.

I yearned for companionship and there seemed to be a curse on my life. I desired a great paying job, but none was to be found. I searched for a route to financial freedom, but I was broke and in debt. I sought after occasions to

Chapter 2: The Journey Ahead

speak and minister to anyone, but doors were closed. Sometimes it seemed with every two steps forward, I was knocked back three. I searched and searched for answers, but could find none except the promises written in the Word of God. Through the Word and a deep commitment to wait on God to perform the impossible, I learned so much about faith and the road ahead, one requiring much patience to travel.

Through a journey of faith, God taught me some important principles I would need to continue my pilgrimage to the other side of life. The Word of God directed me down paths seldom traveled because of the sacrifices one would have to make. Why did I choose to go down the roads I did? At times I don't really know. It would have made much more sense to choose easier paths, but God always gave me enough courage and faith to choose the right direction just when I needed to make a decision.

I received counsel from my pastor at some of the toughest times in my life. I was told I should focus on getting through a night, or perhaps a day, and not to look beyond. There were times when I was so tired of waiting upon the Lord, I would call my pastor and pour out a desperate, lonely, searching heart. He listened and counseled me to look no further than the moments ahead. I learned that moments made up minutes, and minutes made up hours, and hours made up a day, and so forth. When life got so tough, I remember looking to the moments to get through the day.

Other times I felt in my spirit I was taking steps which would benefit me in years to come. I knew certain decisions would take me way into the future. I needed the right directions because to err would be detrimental to things ahead. In those days, God divinely took me by the hand and together we laid a solid foundation, one that I continue to build upon today. Looking back, I know the tough hours were just as important as the giant steps of faith that propelled me to this hour. In all the good times and tough times my faith played a key role.

Over the past years, the Word of God has taught me so much about faith. There were times I needed a slow soaking rain of His truth and God faithfully provided. At times I needed to learn slowly the process of applying faith. On other occasions I just stood firm and heaven moved immediately upon my request. I learned whether prayer was answered then or later, it was still the Lord who answered, and harm never came when I had to patiently wait and wait and wait!

In fact, His Word was the same. I was the same. The circumstances were always different, but the Lord and I didn't change. I grew older, and the Lord added to me wisdom and knowledge. His Word was the same. His promises never wavered. Time continued to pass, and I continued to have faith for what I not only needed from God, but what I wanted as well. Some answers came quickly, while others took time.

Some answers were long coming. Answers I had to wait the longest for gave me time to wonder and question. While I wondered, questioned, and waited, I searched the Word for answers concerning my faith and found that God also answered by saying, "not yet." I examined the things around me, the people around me, and the doctrines I held so dear. I longed to have the answers to all my questions, but in time, God would teach me many truths concerning faith and how to apply it to my life each and every day.

Through time I learned about false faith, quick faith, self faith, and thankfully, real faith. I saw faith exploited for filthy, seemingly righteous, gain. I witnessed lies and hypocrisy by those who seemed to have large followings. I saw the message of faith sold and trampled over by greedy ministers.

No matter what prayer you prayed, or how much you gave, the alarm clock went off on Monday for you to go do the same thing as you did the Friday before – work! Something was wrong with this picture – I just gave a big offering, and/or perhaps I had someone impart faith to me during a prayer on TV, or perhaps someone laid hands on me. Now it was 6:00am and the bills had to be paid, groceries needed to be purchased, and there was yet an eight hour day of sweat to deal with. There was something wrong with this picture, or was there?

Perhaps faith had as much to do with the job, the bills and even the groceries I needed to pick up at the end of the day as it did with the offering made earlier. Could God be concerned about those things as well as the big offering I made to the evangelist and the prayer I received? Were the day-to-day ordeals of life just as important to God, as well as to my faith?

What if faith was so wide and so deep it consumed every part of my life? Could my family play an active role in the faith I would have to build? Was my job an asset to my faith or a liability instead? Did the little insignificant things of this life really play a role in my faith in God? Did God really care who I was, who my friends were, where I lived, what my talents were,

Chapter 2: The Journey Ahead

where I worked? Would these aspects of my life possibly affect my faith at some point?

God taught me through His Word He has been working diligently in my life from the time of conception. Amazingly, He first noticed who I was at that very (seemingly) insignificant moment in my life. Unknown by any person, including my own mother, God started to work in my life and He has never stopped. I was His very precious creation then, and I am still His precious creation today. Time didn't change a thing about how special and miraculous my life was to God then from what it is now. Though I am forty-three years old on this earth, a moment in heaven hasn't even rolled over from the second I began life in my mother's womb.

From that moment in my mother's womb, I would grow and grow. With each passing day after birth, I was to grow in the knowledge of our Lord. This was God's simple little plan for my life then and still is today. The first trust I would place in my parents would be the bedrock to build a foundation of faith in which God would ask me to give Him as well. The same simple faith I would so innocently place in my parents would be transformed into the faith God would use later to move mountains in my life.

Since I jotted down the first word to this book over fourteen years have passed. I have experienced the good, the bad, and the ugly that life has to offer. But God has ministered to me the whole way; and often there was nothing more I could do but to literally trust and obey. There were days that I comforted myself in the fact that God would reward my Faith; however, holding on to God's promises were not always easy.

When I first started writing this book I had nothing materially to claim, just a great family and my unwavering (most of the time) faith in our Lord. Since 1997 I have been married, and now have two precious children. Like all relationships it would be fair to say that the enemy has dealt my wife and me opportunities to grow apart. While I can't say marriage has been easy, I can say we have had to work at it and overcome some of the obstacles with which any Christian couple generally deals.

During the past fourteen years, God opened a door for me to start a business that soon exceeded my wildest expectations. At the height of my business I had 28 employees working in and out of the office serving the needs of the Developmentally Disabled. Business started out great and got better. In time God had blessed me with a wonderful management staff and a wonderful office suite that was envied by most of my competitors.

I soon began to support missionaries from all over the World. I assisted many people with benevolent acts of grace. I sincerely desired to pull everyone I knew up to the level with which I had been blessed. I had many people come into my office to seek counsel in business and personal matters. I literally felt like I was on top of the world. In retrospect, I thought the money would continue to come in -- but soon it came to an end.

At one point my contracts exceeded tens of thousands of dollars a month, and we were growing every day. Instead of putting all the money away and slave-driving my workforce I was generous with what God had given me. Never once did I ever lose sight of God's blessings and my faith in God. My focus on what God had done and what He was going to do through my business never diminished.

Soon clouds appeared on the horizon. Talk of cut backs and change in the Medicaid system began to stir. To be honest, while I knew these things could happen, I never doubted that God would be there with me and continue to increase my business. I really never expected the changes and ultimate fate that awaited me. While I continued to believe and trust in God, I had to sort through the trials and financial realities with which I was now faced.

I pored over the Word and went back to the manuscript of this book searching for where I had failed. I couldn't see God taking away something that was so financially serving of His Kingdom. I wish at this point someone would have given me a copy of the bestseller, <u>Who Moved my Cheese</u>.

In retrospect, God didn't need my money. He wanted me personally involved in ministry for a church I was about to attend. I won't lead you to believe that I was in total understanding and stood unshaken in my faith through this ordeal. I was sifted, refined, and fired through test after test. While it was obvious God was working in my life, I held on to the fact that God must be opening another door since He was closing the door of the business.

During this time, I felt as though God had completely disassembled every piece of my life and expected me to put it all back together again – which is exactly what had to be done. I trusted Him once, but would I trust Him again? Yes, I would trust again; and all the pieces have been going back

Chapter 2: The Journey Ahead

together, right up to the present. Times have been hard. I have searched many hours to find reason for what I perceived as utter madness.

My family went from buying Christmas presents for others, buying groceries for others, and paying for meals for others - to taking canned food back to the store for refunds so we could put gas in the car. I remember buying a glass piggy-bank to start a vacation fund for the children. I had gotten used to putting loose change and even folding a bill or two and wedging it in. One night, in desperation to buy diapers for our daughter, we had no other choice but to take a hammer and break the little glass bank. I even remember on several occasions taking a flash light out to the car at night searching for loose change that had fallen to the floor or between the seats.

Friend, I can't say I understood all of this seemingly financial madness; but despite any present dilemma in which I found myself, I shook my fist toward heaven and exclaimed "I still believe; I will serve you if I have to live in a cardboard box and sell shoe strings to make a living." I found myself frustrated at the Lord and mad at the Devil. By Faith I pressed forward, but I had no vision of what was ahead. I knew that when the day was over I had to trust in the Lord despite any circumstance I found myself in. I remember one night while searching for change in the car floorboard I told God "This isn't how your children are supposed to live – Why God, Why?"

I must admit, if someone would have come up to me in the height of my business and said God wants you to shut it down and go up the road and serve as an Associate Pastor, I would have told them they were foolish and needed to go back and hear from God before they attempted to tell me what He was saying. After all, why would God ask me to shut down a business that was supporting so many ministries and benevolent needs in the community, as well as taking a huge cut in pay and benefits? No, it just didn't make sense.

What was even more interesting was why He needed me at a church where "I" thought everything was as close to perfect as it could get. The Pastor and other ministers and ministries couldn't possibly need anything from me. Little did I know that God was about to transform the entire church where it would never be the same again, and I would become a very close friend and support for the Senior Pastor and take over the administration of the church.

The Lord closed one door while opening a bigger one. He trained me in management with my own business to take over the administration in the church. Even the furniture and office equipment I purchased for my business would be sold for pennies on the dollar to equip our church to give it the image and technology it would need to support the growth God would bring. Today, I clearly see the past and what God was doing the whole time. God is good. In times of uncertainty we must never lose our Faith.

Today, hundreds of miles from where my journey started, I serve as the Pastor of a wonderful community church. The business, the friends, the hurricanes and the never ending work I poured into my previous profession, vocations and Pastorates were all stepping stones to where I am today. Through trial, temptation, and borderline depression, God held me by the hand and led me to a slow, but sure road to victory. Every day I had to apply faith, not faith in faith, faith in myself, or faith in others, but faith in God. My Friend, each precious day of life is another God given opportunity to build our faith as well as encourage and help build another's faith.

Beloved, prepare your heart for the journey ahead. Discover, and emerge victorious over, the good, the bad, and the ugly aspects of faith, fallacy, and fraud..

3 | Outside Of God's Grace

Prayer:

Lord, grant me this hour Knowledge to understand your Word, Wisdom to apply it, Strength that I can bear it, Patience that I can live it, Amen.

One of the greatest steps in understanding God's love toward mankind is being able to comprehend who we are outside of grace. With all due respect, when we consider even our own heart, we find at the center a very fragile and yet hideous person in the light of the Word of God. If you are a Christian, ask yourself this question, "What kind of person would I have been if I would have continued down the same path I was going before I received Christ into my life?" Unfortunately, it takes a lot of guts to be honest with this question. Seriously, once again, without Christ in your life, what kind of person would you be?

Asking sobering questions can often be a painful experience for those of us who may have spent many years on the wild side of life. I know for some, receiving Christ was an opportunity met with open arms at a very young age. However, being saved at a very young age doesn't exclude anyone from the possibilities of how sin may have affected their life.

I realized many years ago the highway to hell offers many decisions. With its paths so wide, the current of sin often takes a person to many extremes while continuing down the river that ultimately feeds into the very gates of hell. One must remember the wide path into hell offers so much to the open-minded.

Chapter 3: Outside of God's Grace

Strangely, as wide as the road to hell is, there really aren't many options to the traveler. Oh, there are a lot of sins one could commit, but remember, according to the Bible, there isn't anything new under the sun. Friend, if you think you're a first, don't flatter yourself, it's been done.

In fact, studies have concluded there are often similar patterns easily tracked for those involved in many types of wickedness. For instance, the drug user may start out as a young rebellious child taking a little smoke every now and then from a cigarette. Later, as peer-pressure mounts, it often turns into a little pot here and there. Unfortunately; most of the time a little pot no longer is enough to pacify, so the child turns to harder drugs to spice things up. By this time, the habit can become a little costly, and most young children are not going to have enough cash flow to support a routine drug habit. What is next? For the child, it becomes a problem of money. "Where am I going to get enough funds to support my habit?" So, he turns to crime.

The next step is usually a little crime here and there to float the bill. Drugs are expensive, and they are not free to the user, only to the beginner. Often drugs are free to those who are trying for their first few times. Pushers know once they have you hooked, they have a customer. Though everyone has a little different edge on their story, the similarities are often shocking. Like I said before, there is nothing new under the sun. Hear the words of Solomon as recorded in the book of Ecclesiastes.

> *The thing that hath been, it is that which shall be; and that which is done is that which shall be done: and there is no new thing under the sun. Is there any thing whereof it may be said, See, this is new? it hath been already of old time, which was before us. (Ecclesiastes 1:9-10)*

I remember years ago having a very sobering thought as I was listening to the news. There was a very shocking story of a hardened criminal that shook the world. This man was considered grossly wicked by even the crudest of sinners. But, I remember what the Holy Spirit spoke to me concerning this man. The Holy Spirit reminded me I could have been this man. This man now faced the death sentence, and it could have been me instead. Friend, you know what else, that man could have been you too. You see, sin is sin as far as our Lord is concerned. God is no respecter of persons.

> *Then Peter opened his mouth, and said, Of a truth I perceive that God is no respecter of persons: But in every nation he that feareth Him, and worketh righteousness, is accepted with Him. (Acts 10:34-35)*

No, I hadn't committed the hideous acts of violence this man had committed. But as a once lost man, I was headed down the same path he was. The options were there for me as well. Some of the options are still there if I will heed the voice of the devil --they are there for you too. Saying no to the devil is easy for many of the temptations he offers, but there are some temptations which seem too great to say no to.

May I ask, what sinful deeds are you hiding deep down inside? How would others accept you if they really knew the sins in your past or the hideous thoughts you have had? Even the sins you placed on the altar years ago, you remember them don't you? What if you had not found Christ? What would your life be like right now?

Beloved, outside of a relationship with God, we have no righteousness. We could never be righteous no matter how hard we try. A man trying to achieve righteousness outside of Christ would only lead himself into despair. Our life is a complete failure outside of grace. Let us look into the Word for what God says about our righteousness.

> *But we are all as an unclean thing, and all our righteousness are as filthy rags; and we all do fade as a leaf; and our iniquities, like the wind, have taken us away. (Isaiah 64:6)*

Friend, that is what the Lord has to say about our righteousness, clearly put as always. But, do we really understand what God is trying to speak to us in this passage? It is absolutely necessary for us to get a clear understanding of who we are, outside of the righteousness we enjoy that is imparted through Christ. If we are ever to understand the magnitude of faith in the life of the Christian, we must first appreciate it, starting with the fact we don't deserve a single thing from God based on our merits.

> *Now it was not written for His sake alone, that it was imputed to Him; But for us also, to whom it shall be imputed, if we believe on Him that raised up Jesus our Lord from the dead; Who was delivered for our offences, and was raised again for our justification. (Romans 4:23-25)*

I believe many have problems understanding faith because of bad education from well-intentioned people who have not a clue about their rightful place in God's eyes both in and outside of grace. Despite great advances of science and technology, we still live in a very ignorant society when it comes to understanding God's wonderful Word. We have been stripped of every possible means, through the fall of man, to do well on our own. We are cursed by the very blood that flows through our veins.

Chapter 3: Outside of God's Grace

> *The fool hath said in his heart, There is no God. They are corrupt, they have done abominable works, there is none that doeth good. (Psalms 14:1)*

Below are two passages from the Word dealing with the righteousness of man, one from each Testament of the Bible.

> *The fool hath said in his heart, There is no God. Corrupt are they, and have done abominable iniquity: there is none that doeth good. God looked down from heaven upon the children of men, to see if there were any that did understand, that did seek God. Every one of them is gone back: they are altogether become filthy; there is none that doeth good, no, not one. (Psalms 53:1-3)*

> *As it is written, There is none righteous, no, not one: There is none that understandeth, there is none that seeketh after God. They are all gone out of the way, they are together become unprofitable; there is none that doeth good, no, not one. (Romans 3:10-12)*

Let's go back to the beginning of creation and take an in-depth look at things around the first family's home. Remember, there are two perfect beings in the Garden of Eden. God has blessed them and made them after His own image. Adam and Eve are as pure as pure can be. They are spotless in the eyes of a holy and just God.

As you know by now, the devil literally despises all things pure and holy. You might say that purity and righteousness are antonyms of wickedness and corruption. This is the reason the devil goes after young girls and boys to throw their virginity down the drain. Through television and the media, education and various programs, Satan has lied to the public and replaced lust for love. Adam and Eve knew and experienced purity of heart, mind, and soul, but they traded it for a lie, just as millions of people are sadly doing today. Beloved, listening to the devil will cost you dearly.

Now, Eve listens to the devil and she is deceived by his wicked lies. Then, Adam listens to his beguiled wife and deliberately disobeys God's Word. Adam and Eve have really put themselves in a bind. They chose to believe the rotten lies of a serpent over a God who came and visited them like a neighbor in the cool of the day. They sacrificed more on that day than they ever knew, for the simple gratification of flesh. I wonder what we have sacrificed on the altars of self, to gratify our flesh for a moment of pleasure.

Next, the Bible takes us deeper into the lives of our first parents. With earth recently created, the Bible ushers the reader right into a family spat that turns tragic. According to the Bible Adam and Eve now have two sons. What could possibly top the trouble Adam and Eve got themselves (and us) into in the Garden? Out of four people on the whole earth, two are already in trouble with the Lord. Let us see what will happen to the two children.

> *And Cain talked with Abel his brother: and it came to pass, when they were in the field, that Cain rose up against Abel his brother, and slew him. And the LORD said unto Cain, Where is Abel thy brother? And he said, I know not: Am I my brother's keeper? And He said, What hast thou done? the voice of thy brother's blood crieth unto me from the ground. And now art thou cursed from the earth, which hath opened her mouth to receive thy brother's blood from thy hand; (Genesis 4:8-11)*

What? Now we are down from four to only three occupying the earth. One man kills one fourth of earth's population. Abel, a good man, and by all implications a very devout one, is murdered. At this point in history, there are three mentioned persons, all of whom have been sentenced in some way by the Lord. Friend, if that doesn't convince you of the unrighteousness of man, maybe this next passage will.

Two chapters later and six chapters into the Word of God, we discover that things on earth have gotten pretty wicked; we now have gone from bad to worse. From three very troubled individuals in chapter four, to the whole earth being filled with wickedness, God is now faced with a situation that must be dealt with. It is hard to believe that earth, in such a short time since creation, could possibly be in the sinful condition that it is.

Beloved, you are witnessing the pitiful state of man without God. We have seen what would be a candid picture of ourselves without God's Grace. We are seeing our neighbors across the street who desperately need the Lord in their lives. Maybe it is that co-worker to whom you may need to present the Gospel. For any generation of people to expect to have done better in those tragic days of old, the overwhelming evidence is mounting up to challenge any such notion. Let us take a look at how things are shaping up in Genesis chapter six.

> *And God saw that the wickedness of man was great in the earth, and that every imagination of the thoughts of his heart was only evil continually. And it repented the LORD that He had made man on the earth, and it grieved Him at His heart. And the LORD said, I will destroy man whom I have created from the face of the earth; both man, and*

Chapter 3: Outside of God's Grace

beast, and the creeping thing, and the fowls of the air; for it repenteth Me that I have made them. (Genesis 6:5-7)

It is sad a man must put himself through this understanding of who he is in relationship to a holy, righteous and awesome God, but it is absolutely necessary in order to realize the pathetic sinfulness of mortal man as he reaches out for God's mercy. I have noticed lately, in what is supposed to be Bible believing Churches, a real trend of departing from this fundamental point. Many preachers and teachers of the Gospel like to hide the point I am trying to make. Why, because it is not popular to accuse one of such deceitful wickedness.

When families drive off from a fine suburban home in their SUV and pull up to the First Church, many do not want to hear the truth about their soul. Man does not want a preacher to look him in the eye and with a heart of compassion but an unction to tell the truth say, "Sir, Ma'am, you are a shameful mess and on your way to a devil's Hell, without the sin cleansing blood of Jesus Christ." Unfortunately, people often choose to squelch out the authority of God's Word and weaken it to pageantries and programs, openly denying their heart is desperately wicked.

I must conclude a message on the condition of man's soul does seem to rub the wrong way; after all, we are accustomed to having things our way, aren't we? Burger King once ran ads declaring "Have it Your Way". I think the church responded to this marketing strategy and rearranged its tolerance concerning the sinful nature of man.

The truth is, when you remind a person of the condition of his soul without the presence of a Savior abiding within, it is a direct assault on pride – that's right – PRIDE! The fact of each man, woman, and even child having to deal with a fallen nature often goes against the grain of what we are being taught in our classrooms and living rooms each day and night. With the liberal self-serving pseudo-theology, it makes it hard for people to face up to the fact we cannot save ourselves because we are wicked in the sight of a holy God. Hollywood certainly goes to great trouble to defy this fundamental doctrine.

The reason Humanism is so attractive to our society, is because humanism says you are in control. You decide your fate. There are no absolutes. Everything is relative. You are your own truth. You are your own god. This is ridiculous nonsense and poison that is being perpetrated to our children every day at many schools and at home on the television. God's Word declares the human race as lost, defiled, and separated from any righteousness.

The sad point in Genesis six is: the Bible says ...that every imagination of the thoughts of his heart was only evil continually. The word continually is used here to drive the point home without misunderstanding. The imagination and wickedness of man's heart was not "often" times evil, "part" of the time evil, or even "most" of the time evil; but the word says continually evil, ALL day, ALL night, ALL week, ALL year, etc.

I cannot imagine what could have been so evil during the days of Noah to cause God to destroy the earth, especially when I look at the evil parading itself on our streets, in our markets, and across the television each day. We often make the comment, "I don't know if it can get any worse". Perhaps it will get a lot worse than it is now – who knows what tomorrow holds, we just know who holds it – Amen?

When I consider the story of Sodom and Gomorrah's tragic end, I often ask myself just how far are we from such judgment. What will it take to trigger the judgment of God? What event, what trend, what law, will be the straw that breaks the camel's back? It seems our society studies evil continually as well. Our communities are filled with corruption from the top of society to the bottom, from the aristocrat to the pauper. Will it get worse? My friend, it has to.

Did you know geography places the Dead Sea over what were once Sodom and Gomorrah? God does have an unusual and creative way of dealing with sin and wicked cultures, doesn't He? I wonder what will be the case today. Not only does the Dead Sea cover those once great cities, but to add insult to injury, Sodom and Gomorrah are the lowest natural ground elevations on the face of the earth - What a testimony! To add further insult, the sea that covers those two great cities is so salty it will not sustain sea life, unlike what we find in every other body of water.

What causes a society to indulge in such blatant sin? It seems that man, for once, would learn a lesson from history if he is not going to learn it from God. The fact is, he cannot understand the truth nor is it possible for him to live free from sin outside of Grace. Man's problem is his heart. Man's heart is black with sin and he has a sinful nature that keeps him separated from God's presence.

> *The heart is deceitful above all things, and desperately wicked: who can know it? I the LORD search the heart, I try the reins, even to give every*

> man according to his ways, and according to the fruit of his doings. (Jeremiah 17:9-10)

Consider this verse very carefully; look at what the English is telling you and me about the heart. The Bible does not indicate the heart is bad, mean, rough, or unkind; it says it is deceitful. Not just a little or a lot or sometimes or most of the time, but deceitful above all things. Now, that is a sobering statement to make in light of our modern "psycho crazed media cure all culture". You can bet one thing, there isn't a pill or therapy that can cure this problem, no matter what a doctor may tell you, Jesus is the cure.

Just what is meant by the word deceitful according to the Hebrew? The deep meaning of the word is fraudulent, which has as its root a word meaning to swell up. It almost appears to suggest the word pride. Imagine the nature of our heart being fraudulent. The meaning also takes on the word crooked and polluted. You know the Word of God drives a hard bargain when dealing with man's true condition. I believe so much could be solved if the whole world could grasp the true Biblical understanding of man's heart.

Not only is the heart deceitful above all things, but the passage goes on to say "...and desperately wicked: who can know it?" It seems that with all that is aligned against man's heart, the Bible would offer some relief, but not just yet. Man is certainly down for the count here in this passage. Desperately is a very strong word in any text. In fact this is the only time the word is even used in the whole (KJV) Bible, which in itself should send a message.

Jeremiah, writing under the inspiration of the Holy Spirit, certainly gets the point conveyed to the reader. We don't have to know Hebrew to figure out what God was trying to say about the heart of man. However, just the same, I want to go ahead and share the definition of desperately wicked. The root of the word means to be frail and feeble; figuratively it means incurable, sick, and woeful.

Without a doubt that's certainly the condition of our heart, incurable without the blood of Jesus Christ. I know it is unfortunate without Christ there is no hope for mankind, but through the Gospel hope is promised to everyone who would believe on the saving name of Jesus Christ. What was once a tragic story for man's own attempt to find hope in this world turns out to be not so dismal after all. The problem with many is - they will not submit themselves to the Word of God and accept themselves for who they really are - feeble and incurable, and their every attempt for righteousness is fraudulent.

Fortunately, with this chapter in mind, man is now ready to move on to brighter things. Greener pastures are just in sight with the understanding of man's heart outside of grace. It is paramount that we absolutely understand all of our attempts for righteousness are in vain and will be of no merit before an omnipotent, omniscient, righteous, and holy God.

Let's recap a bit. We are desperately wicked, a miserable wreck and worthless apart from the atonement we receive through the shed blood of Jesus Christ, our soon coming King. If a man, woman, or child is lost, they have no hope in this life apart from the convicting, wooing power of the Holy Spirit pointing to the cross. Their heart is predisposed to sin, making them come into this life as a guilty unrighteous sinner in search of gratifying all of his or her earthly immoral desires.

The point of this chapter is to demonstrate the lack of any good you and I can accomplish on our own. Through Salvation, God grants us the righteousness of His Son Jesus Christ. When we stand before God, we stand clothed in another's robe of righteousness, not our own.

In relation to faith, we would have to conclude it is impossible for us to have faith in ourselves or any other person who is not made righteous through the soul cleansing power of the Blood. For any who have not been justified before a holy, righteous God, we cannot put one ounce of faith in them. Nor can we even put faith in ourselves, when what we seek to accomplish is not subject to, or under the authority of, the righteousness of Christ.

In conclusion, the scriptures are adamant; there is no good in people who are outside of Grace. Outside of Grace, there is no hope, no functional FAITH that has power to transform a life. Faith outside of Christ does no good, has no value and has no power to change our life nor those around us.

Prayer:

Father in heaven, help us clearly understand our position outside of Your Grace. Let us understand we are nothing outside of our relationship with You through Jesus Christ your Only Begotten Son. We joyously celebrate the righteousness that has been divinely imparted to us by a work we could have never done, a work we did not deserve. Help us to always be mindful of the manifold blessings we have obtained through Your abundant riches, endless love, and tender mercy. Let me rejoice daily in Your Grace. Amen.

4 | Man's Created Purpose

The procedure of understanding faith and applying it to our life involves the clear absolute comprehension of the nature and purpose of our creation. Without man having a biblical cognition of his post in God's creation, he will never be able to comprehend the bumps, turns, heartbreaks, and tragedies of this life. There is no doubt in my mind (as a minister) a comprehensive understanding of the reason of our existence will, and can, change our perspective of others and ourselves.

As we move toward understanding faith we must establish this essential truth; we are an absolute, indispensable part of God's identity. Follow me slowly; through man God demonstrates and communicates Himself to others. Not only do the heavens declare His glory, but it is our purpose to reflect the glory of God as well. We are not to reflect our own vain and selfish purposes.

We were not created to live merely to obtain and attain great riches before our fellow man. The Bible does not declare in the Lord's Prayer, "...our will be done in earth as it is in heaven", the prayer goes "*Thy will be done.*" In fact it is not a request; it is a command. As children of God we have a responsibility to worship and glorify the Lord. Even Jesus Himself told His disciples if we cease to praise Him, the rocks would cry out. Consider these passages below.

> *Sing unto the LORD, all the earth; show forth from day to day His salvation. Declare His glory among the heathen; His marvelous works among all nations. For great is the LORD, and greatly to be praised: He*

Chapter 4: Man's Created Purpose

also is to be feared above all gods. For all the gods of the people are idols: but the LORD made the heavens. Glory and honour are in His presence; strength and gladness are in His place. Give unto the LORD, ye kindreds of the people, give unto the LORD glory and strength. Give unto the LORD the glory due unto His name: bring an offering, and come before Him: worship the LORD in the beauty of holiness. (1 Chronicles 16: 23-29)

The heavens declare the glory of God; and the firmament showeth His handywork. Day unto day uttereth speech, and night unto night showeth knowledge. There is no speech nor language, where their voice is not heard. (Psalms 19:1)

The LORD reigneth; let the earth rejoice; let the multitude of isles be glad thereof. Clouds and darkness are round about Him: righteousness and judgment are the habitation of His throne. A fire goeth before Him, and burneth up His enemies round about. His lightnings enlightened the world: the earth saw, and trembled. The hills melted like wax at the presence of the LORD, at the presence of the Lord of the whole earth. The heavens declare His righteousness and all the people see His glory. (Psalms 97:1-6)

God's perfect will is unmistakable; it hasn't changed from the dawning of early creation. His will and aspiration for each created man, woman, and child has never changed.

The Responsibility of Man

I am always amazed at the frivolous rationale of Christians, who think God changes his mind every twenty years or so, and those who perhaps accept the unfortunate false indoctrination of the "new thing" theology perpetrated largely by mega media ministry giants and churches leaning more often toward a charismatic persuasion.

While it is certain we live in a fast paced society consumed with upgrading its gadgets, changing its habits, clothes, and interests every time a hit movie is released, we should never associate faddish and unstable behavior with the character of our Lord -- the "Ancient of Days."

Sadly, "New Thing" ideology has rooted deep in many of our churches. Such instability and uncertainty must be carefully extracted from our congregations. Strangely, many of today's Christians view God as one who is anxiously equipping Himself to fit into this modern, sophisticated on-line society. People change. Styles come and go. Culture continuously changes, but God is the same. The Faith it took for Peter to walk on water hasn't changed a bit. Redemption is still through the Blood of Jesus. Ministers and laypersons will continue to search for fresh messages and current illustrations, but the fundamentals of our Faith are solid and unchanged.

We know God's laws have never changed nor suffered conflict because of our advancement into the future. All knowledge comes from God, and no matter how technical our world becomes, we will never be able to comprehend God's awesome power. There will be those who will try, but to their own dismay, they will never come within a million miles of understanding a God who simply spoke things into existence, One who simply scraped up the dirt of the ground and made man, who then, out of all things, took a rib out of His creation and made a woman.

Beloved, we must understand God is still the same. The Word is still as relevant as it has always been. We change our mind so much we often have no idea what we want out of life, where we want to live, what we want to drive, and on and on, but God's Word is complete and absolute truth down to the dotted "i". We do not live in a time when the Word should be discarded as irrelevant for our generation. In fact, there has never been a better time for someone to stand firmly and proclaim "thus saith the Lord" in our homes, our communities, our churches, our schools, and our government offices. God's promises are as relevant today as they were four thousand years ago.

We are the prized creation of God. We are to exemplify the very character of God to all men in all parts of the earth. Animals cannot take the Gospel to the four corners of the earth, but we can, and we must. If you want to comprehend the epitome of what man is to become on this earth, we must start with understanding our Lord and His divine plan for our life. We are not gods, but we are made in the likeness and image of God. We do not become gods, but we may receive Him into our life. We, as God's most prized creation, are to reflect the following in our lives:

God's Comfort
Blessed be God, even the Father of our Lord Jesus Christ, the Father of mercies, and the God of all comfort; Who comforteth us in all our tribulation, that we may be able to comfort them which are in any trouble, by the comfort wherewith we ourselves are comforted of God. (2 Corinthians 1:3-4)

God's Faithfulness

I will sing of the mercies of the LORD for ever: with my mouth will I make known Thy faithfulness to all generations. For I have said, Mercy shall be built up for ever: Thy faithfulness shalt Thou establish in the very heavens. I have made a covenant with My chosen, I have sworn unto David My servant, Thy seed will I establish for ever, and build up thy throne to all generations. Selah. And the heavens shall praise Thy wonders, O LORD: Thy faithfulness also in the congregation of the saints. For who in the heaven can be compared unto the LORD? who among the sons of the mighty can be likened unto the LORD? God is greatly to be feared in the assembly of the saints, and to be had in reverence of all them that are about Him. O LORD God of Hosts, who is a strong LORD like unto Thee? or to Thy faithfulness round about Thee? (Psalms 89:1-8)

God's Forbearance
Beareth all things, believeth all things, hopeth all things, endureth all things. (1 Corinthians 13:7)

God's Forgiveness
(And their sins and iniquities will I remember no more. (Hebrews 10:17)

God's Grace
He hath made His wonderful works to be remembered: the LORD is gracious and full of compassion. (Psalms 111:4)

God's Holiness
Let them praise Thy great and terrible name; for it is holy. The king's strength also loveth judgment; Thou dost establish equity, Thou executest judgment and righteousness in Jacob. Exalt ye the LORD our God, and worship at His footstool; for He is holy. (Psalms 99:3-5)

God's Love and Patience
Charity suffereth long, and is kind; charity envieth not; charity vaunteth not itself, is not puffed up, (1 Corinthians 13:4)

God's Wisdom
Who is a wise man and endued with knowledge among you? let him show out of a good conversation his works with meekness of wisdom. But the wisdom that is from above is first pure, then peaceable, gentle,

and easy to be entreated, full of mercy and good fruits, without partiality, and without hypocrisy. (James 3:13,17)

It was man's inaugural purpose to make evident God's existence – not the picturesque creation our eyes observe each time we gaze across the heavens and earth. You and I are to demonstrate through a faithful life the very character of our Creator. Today's environmentalists have it all wrong, the earth does not illustrate the character of God, we do!

Humans received their soul from the Creator, not creation. God gave us responsibility over the earth. Creation is not responsible for itself, nor is it responsible for man. We are to dominate the earth and make use of its resources; which includes cutting trees, drilling for oil, and killing animals for food and other uses.

However, we do have a responsibility to take care of the earth, to not abuse and destroy the things God has given to us. Man is to be a warden of the things of this earth. Shortly after creation God charged man with a set of instructions for proper maintenance and stewardship of this earth. In Genesis One, we find this relevant passage:

And God blessed them, and God said unto them, Be fruitful, and multiply, and replenish the earth, and subdue it: and have dominion over the fish of the sea, and over the fowl of the air, and over every living thing that moveth upon the earth. And God said, Behold, I have given you every herb bearing seed, which is upon the face of all the earth, and every tree, in the which is the fruit of a tree yielding seed; to you it shall be for meat. And to every beast of the earth, and to every fowl of the air, and to every thing that creepeth upon the earth, wherein there is life, I have given every green herb for meat: and it was so. And God saw every thing that He had made, and, behold, it was very good. And the evening and the morning were the sixth day. (Genesis 1:28-31)

Evidence of man's abuse of the earth cannot be ignored, but that in itself is in opposition to the character we were created to reflect. True, with the sin curse, man was alienated from the initial qualities he first possessed, but that is not God's fault, it is ours. Man has slowly walked away from God's Word and ignored the commands of the Lord. We have no one to blame but ourselves for the problems we face. You will not find one scripture giving humanity the right to abuse and waste one part of the divine creation. Our instructions are clearly outlined in the preceding passage.

Chapter 4: Man's Created Purpose

Man's problem is overcoming his innate desire to fulfill his own will instead of God's. We challenge the Lord daily with our own stubborn intentions and reckless decisions. We fail to consider the long-term consequences that are wrought through our determination to gratify our selfish desires. For us to live victoriously, we must come to terms with our created purpose. When we choose to surrender to a higher calling, rather than conceding to the will and wishes of mortal family and friends around us, we will be able to accomplish great things for the Kingdom of God.

Mankind will never be content with himself as long as he functions outside of the will of God. Peace in the home, the work-place, the streets, and the schools will never be achieved as long as man continues to satisfy his own self-seeking desires rather than forfeiting his fallen sin nature and giving over to the will of God. The decisions are ones he must make for himself; the result is a positive, life-changing experience not only for himself and his close loved ones, but also for the community around him.

When man decides to forfeit his will and submit wholeheartedly to God, will life be a bed of roses? Absolutely not; however, life will be increasingly rewarding, and all you do will be safeguarded by the miraculous providence of God. Friend, stop fighting God's battles. Let the Lord fight His own battles. By you submitting to the total will of God, it puts Him responsible for clearing paths you and I could never do alone. If you are a willing vessel for God to use, there is nothing that can stand in your way. Victory is your destiny as long as God is in full control of your life.

One practical and necessary step for you to make right now is finding contentment in your divine purpose. It is time to die to your own desires and let God take control of your life. You might say to yourself, "I don't want to surrender my will to God. I want to accomplish goals I have set for myself," or perhaps you're saying, "I have a rewarding career and I don't have time to be involved in all that church stuff." Are you afraid that God may want you to do something seemingly foolish, or give up something for which you have worked so hard?

Beloved, implementing the purpose of God will take you places you never thought possible. You will be happier than you have ever been in your life. You will get better sleep and rest easier, knowing God Himself is in total control of your life. Of course there will be those days things might not go like you planned; however, contentment will fill your heart and flood your soul despite anything that comes your way.

Over the years I have watched a lot of people reach a point in their life where they had no other choice but to surrender to God's will. Their situation had reached such a low point that further digression would have led to foolish decisions such as drugs, psychotic behavior, and perhaps, the contemplation of suicide. As we sink into the depression of failure, the ground around us begins to close in. What used to be light around us is replaced by darkness of every kind.

Then, suddenly, we begin to feel that last perk of strength and by the power of the Holy Spirit we glance up one last time and see the light of day shining brightly above our head. We muster up that last ounce of energy and slowly reach toward the heavens, then from out of nowhere descends the ever-present hand of God, and He begins to pull us out of our pit. As we cling tightly to His hand and surrender, the shackles and fetters that had us bound begin to break away and fall beneath us.

I confess; sometimes I get a little tired of watching others achieve their earthly desires – a new car, things around the house, vacations, etc. etc. etc… But friend, I know I am standing dead center of where God wants me to be at this point in my life. In the spirit, I have no regrets about what I should have done yesterday or fears about what tomorrow will hold. In the flesh there are often occurrences of fear and unbelief that must be crucified. Then, to add insult to injury, the unfaithful few (certain friends and family members) are always there to misguide and discourage your pilgrimage toward victorious living.

My friend, you are on your way to understanding a cornerstone truth of faith. I say "Cornerstone," because now you realize you must surrender your desires and take on the purpose of your creation. You must submit to God's will instead of your own. As long as a person is in direct submission to the will of God, he or she is untouchable. God is the final authority. As long as He is using you to fulfill His purpose, you will sustain life, as well as endure to the end of your life's journey. Moreover, you will always have the necessities to accomplish His purpose. As long as you are accomplishing God's will in your life, you are indestructible.

Beloved, as you travel down this path, you will have food and shelter to sustain life, and clothes to cover your body so you can present yourself modestly. You will have transportation to travel to places the Lord will require of you. In short, if you're going to work, than work for the Lord, and let Him pay the way. Don't try and do it yourself. Trying to make your own way will only lead to despair. One pastor summed it up best when he said, "Stop trying, and start trusting".

You have a purpose on this earth. Your purpose is to ultimately glorify God through the gifts and talents God has given each of us. Our own paths and desires will lead us to despair unless we allow the Lord to take what we enjoy and bring it into a purpose God can use in and through us. To diligently apply faith to our own selfishly desired purpose is to set ourselves up for ultimate failure and consternation; however, to apply our faith in what our true purpose as God intended it to be, is to secure absolute victory in our life despite the bumps ahead of us.

To take on the character of God is to likely set yourself up to be a total disappointment to many (including family and loved ones) around you. Your popularity will diminish as your faith transforms you into a surrendered vessel for God to use as He sees fit for the expansion of the Kingdom of God. As you take on Christ-like behavior and obedience, you will never lack for anything to accomplish God's work. God will keep you healthy and blessed to accomplish His will.

Your faith will work seamlessly as you apply it to fulfilling God's purpose in your life instead of falling for the popular entitlement Gospel that is so often preached in our churches. Wrestling with God is futile. Exercise faith in what you know God wants for your life. Faith on your part, coupled with total surrender to fulfill God's will in your life is certain victory – You cannot lose.

Prayer:

Lord, I do want to live a fulfilling life on this earth, but I realize my ways are not Your ways. My desires are not Your desires. I don't have the peace of mind I should. I am not content with the way I am living. Lord, grant me the faith I need to release my will, and the strength and courage I need to submit myself, to Your divine purpose. I do want to radiate Your glory. I want to reflect Your holiness, faithfulness, grace, love, patience, forbearance, comfort, forgiveness, and wisdom to the entire world. I want the whole world to see You inside of me. Lord, help me to die, so You might live out Your perfect will through me. Help me to be ever conscious of Your purpose for my existence. Amen.

5 | Man's Duties In The Garden

Now man was not created and placed in the garden without instructions; God was sure to put him to work. Some have the idea that God just decided to create man and woman, give them a few parameters, and let them run free on the planet like the beasts of the field. What a misconception of creation as recorded in scripture!

Always remember this fact: God is a God of economy! GOD CREATES ALL THINGS WITH TOTAL PURPOSE. Everything created has a perfect place, right down to the falling star on a moonlit night.

Let's consider what the Bible has to say on this point:

> *To every thing there is a season, and a time to every purpose under the heaven: A time to be born, and a time to die; a time to plant, and a time to pluck up that which is planted; A time to kill, and a time to heal; a time to break down, and a time to build up; A time to weep, and a time to laugh; a time to mourn, and a time to dance; A time to cast away stones, and a time to gather stones together; a time to embrace, and a time to refrain from embracing; A time to get, and a time to lose; a time to keep, and a time to cast away; A time to rend, and a time to sew; a time to keep silence, and a time to speak; A time to love, and a time to hate; a time of war, and a time of peace. (Ecclesiastes 3:1-8)*

To be very candid, the first thing God actually did after He created man was put him to work. Yes, that is right, work. It was a time of Work! God has never meant for man to loaf around on this earth from place to place dodging responsibility. Our modern culture would do well to understand this powerful concept in their divinely created purpose.

It is for certain we live in a day where fewer people are willing to work, but everyone wants to get rich. The dead-beat and/or get-rich-quick mentality is clearly evident with our state sponsored lotteries, legalized gambling, and further propagated with government sponsored handouts. In Old and New Testament times, if a man didn't work, he didn't eat.

> *For even when we were with you, this we commanded you, that if any would not work, neither should he eat. For we hear that there are some which walk among you disorderly, working not at all, but are busybodies. (2 Thessalonians. 3:10-11)*

One unknown author puts it this way: "Work is man's great function. He is nothing, he can do nothing, he can achieve nothing, fulfill nothing, without working. If you are poor—work. If you are rich—continue working. If you are burdened with seemingly unfair responsibilities—work. If you are happy, keep right on working. Idleness gives room for doubt and fears. If disappointments come—work. If your health is threatened—work. When faith falters—work. When dreams are shattered and hope seems dead—work. Work as if your life were in peril. It really is. No matter what ails you—work. Work faithfully—work with faith. Work is the greatest remedy available for mental and physical afflictions."

Today we reward the rebellion of men and women who choose not to work with entitlements of every kind. We have government programs to accommodate the most slothful of people. In fact I would submit to you many programs are purposely designed to reward those who choose to be couch-potatoes. It is anti-Christian to support such programs because it is a deliberate assault on Scripture.

I would like to commend those who have worked diligently to rewrite and legislate new programs rewarding those who would actively seek employment during their time of trouble. There is a big push in several states to abolish the old system that merely locked people into a welfare program without giving them the necessary assistance to get out of such a rut later.

Years ago I had a great job at a mission where I was given the responsibility of providing shelter and food for many who were in serious financial trouble. During that time I realized after a good bit of questioning, often the people who approached me for assistance were lazy, selfish, greedy, irresponsible and sinful people who rebelled against submission to any and all authority, including the ultimate authority – God. There were those who were genuinely in need of help because of a variety of problems in their life, and I was always eager to assist them in any capacity possible. I have been desperate myself and I hope I never forget what it was like as long as I live.

Often when I had the opportunity to minister to transients, the Word of God would pierce deep through to their heart and some would repent of their sins, confess Christ as Savior and change their whole mentality often within hours, a remarkable change would occur without the help of a psychologist, career services, or daytime television talk shows, just the simple Gospel of Jesus Christ and applied faith on their part.

Sadly, for many of the transients I ministered to, their battle was quickly identified as submitting to authority. They rebelled against authority as a child, they couldn't stand community ordinances, and they despised having to obey regulations and knowing the police were ultimately going to enforce compliance. Many would cause problems while staying at the mission by failing to simply follow a few rules. If you said, "Stand here," they wanted to stand there. If they were to sit and wait, they wanted to stand and complain.

Over the past I have had the opportunity to manage a few businesses and I have noticed the same problem exists in the workplace as well. If you needed a paper turned in on a certain date, it didn't matter; there would be those who would have a sack of excuses as to why they couldn't comply. Much of the time it would be the same people having problems over and over with authority.

Before moving on I would like to make a statement, Christians that love and honor the authority of God do not have a problem respecting and submitting in the workplace as well. Those who argue and seek to thwart the authority in a work environment are surely to take their attitude into the church and do the same before the Pastor and ultimately before God. As we move forward in faith we must keep ourselves separated from those to whom the enemy would have us fall victim. God wants us to be submissive to those in authority. By doing so it will be a testimony of our love and obedience to God. We will be a role model for others to follow, and in many cases, an open door to be a witness for our Lord.

Chapter 5: Man's Duties In The Garden

As we can see according to God's infallible Word, man was given the task of dressing and keeping the garden. Notice God confronts man with his responsibility before He gives him the "dos & don'ts". Remember, God is an economic God. God does not waste his created resources. If God created you, you have a purpose. If God has given you talent, He expects you to use it. By the way, this rule never changes.

I want us to look at the word "dress". If God created Man and created this complete bio system for man to sustain life, then why was man to dress the garden? You might be asking yourself, with all due respect, it seems God has already taken care of everything. Don't be so quick my friend. With life comes serious responsibility. Despite that horrifying word in this generation, God demands RESPONSIBILITY. It is not asked or pleaded of Him- it is a command.

Unfortunately, this free-ride mentality has found its way into our churches and behind the pulpits. I have heard a stomach-full of false preaching on the subject of Salvation. So many times you hear messages urging people to just come and confess, but the new creature is aborted on conception. The word "Repent" is hardly used behind pulpits and in Christian circles. As we accept Christ there must be a change of some kind. If a person continues down the same road as before and returns to the same places, the same friends, and the same ways, there is no change. And with that, you insult the Spirit of God who is working the miracle of Salvation.

In addition to change there will come a natural desire to move closer to the Lord. In time the desire will lead to deeper and deeper love for the Lord and His work. While we all can't be pastors or missionaries, there will be plenty of work to be done in the local church. A good pastor will foster a love for his flock to serve in many capacities, and not just limited to the local church. The idea here is not a works-salvation; it is a desire to love God in ways that exceed a one-time verbal confession of acceptance.

The root of the Hebrew word 'abad, means to work. We get the full meaning of the word as defined: to serve or till. We were given the responsibility to till the soil in the garden. Now, as far as how much physical labor was involved, we can only guess it was more time consuming than labor. Reasoning is supported by the fact man was cursed to work by the sweat of his brow after the fall in the garden. In any sense, we must conclude God put man to work immediately, no matter what the severity of labor might have been. In addition to putting man to work, God provided all that was necessary for man to accomplish this task in the garden.

Fortunately, for us Christians, the Holy Spirit is there to make intercession for us, and we have ample support to make our requests known to God. We further know all we need to do is to speak to God and He is there to answer and even listen to our heart's desire. I wonder how much time we spend letting God know our needs instead of our wants?

Did you know God stands ready to equip you with everything it takes to accomplish that which He has willed you to do, all He has called you to do? You need only to submit yourself to His will and all things will be given to you. We are talking about everyday APPLIED FAITH, no fanfare, no bells or whistles, no magic needed, no prayer lines, no words from a prophet, no seed offerings, no faith pledges, just a submissive spirit to the will of God in our day to day lives. You might be telling yourself, "I don't farm." Maybe not, but whatever the responsibilities God has given you, He will be there to assist you in completing that task.

I don't farm either; however, I need Him all the same. If I need Him to help me fix an engine because I am a mechanic, then He is there to impart the wisdom and knowledge needed. God knows all things; He is hip on all things no matter what the details or circumstances are. God wants us to use the resources He has given us to do the jobs He has called us to. Jobs outside of church work are just as important to God as those which encircle the church. A promotion in the work place is as important as an expanding nursery ministry in the church.

Think of it this way. Suppose for a moment God never cared about the things that took place outside our home and the church. Where would the finances come from if we needed to add on to the church, pay the staff, and buy new equipment? Does that money just happen to be in the bank account every month? No. Somebody has to go outside the church and gain that money through a job and then pay a tithe or give an offering for the church to afford to make the appropriate purchases.

Your new raise at work is vital to the Kingdom of God. The Lord is behind you doing a great job at work and earning that needed promotion. While it is for certain God owns the cattle on a thousand hills and the hills as well, He has set forth a system for this creation to obtain material gain. It comes through work or inheritance and/ or gifts. Coincidentally, if we didn't work for our money ourselves, you can rest assured our gifts or inheritances came from the labors of someone else.

Chapter 5: Man's Duties In The Garden

I want you to understand something about our Lord; He is not ignorant regarding our culture. We often think of God as being too distant to understand the current issues of life. We often think of the Bible as being out-of-date and out-of-touch with society's problems. The real problem is - you and I are the ones who are out-of-touch, and we are often out-of-touch concerning God's Word.

God is not out-of-touch, neither is His Word. In fact, though things may seem a little technical these days, they are certainly no different than they have always been. People have been scamming and conniving since creation. God's Word is full of stories describing events that parallel with today's headline news. The Bible is as relevant as it was five hundred years ago. The Word of God is as up to date as it was in the desert on the way to the Promise Land.

Solomon writes in Ecclesiastes:

> *One generation passeth away, and another generation cometh: but the earth abideth for ever. The sun also ariseth, and the sun goeth down, and hasteth to his place where he arose. The wind goeth toward the south, and turneth about unto the north; it whirleth about continually, and the wind returneth again according to his circuits. All the rivers run into the sea; yet the sea is not full; unto the place from whence the rivers come, thither they return again. All things are full of labour; man cannot utter it: the eye is not satisfied with seeing, nor the ear filled with hearing. The thing that hath been, it is that which shall be; and that which is done is that which shall be done: and there is no new thing under the sun. Is there any thing whereof it may be said, See, this is new? it hath been already of old time, which was before us.* (Ecclesiastes 1:4-10)

Friend, not only is there nothing new under the sun, but there is nothing new about God. He is there to help us have the things we need. Yes, He may have charged man to till the earth then, but what is He charging you with today? Ask yourself this sobering question: Lord, what do you want out of me this day? What can I do to fulfill your purpose in my life? Where do you want me to Work? What kind of career can I have that will bring honor and glory to your name? How can I include you in my work and be a blessing to those around my office or in my workplace?

In those early days man worked to survive by making sure there was another meal in the ground for tomorrow. It is true we have the big super markets to purchase nicely packaged food items. God understands the cultural changes people have made and allows for them as well. In order to be responsible, God may have you working as a welder, air-traffic controller, a nurse; however, the demand is still the same. Your responsibility hasn't changed a bit. We all have a workload. God is there to help you.

Have you ever noticed those people holding signs up at busy intersection? I am always a little amused at what many of the signs read, such as "Work for Food." It dawned on me one day that I was working for the same reason. Perhaps the way some of us go about it is little more sophisticated than the sign, but it's still the same --work. Hard, rigorous, sometimes sweaty; that's work.

We love to have nice things in our home, but it is still shelter to us. Money spent for food at a fancy restaurant still provides food no matter how you slice it. We spend a lot of money on designer clothes, but they still cover our nakedness, or at least they are supposed to.

Our work is VERY important to God and is necessary for a proper relationship with our Lord. God wants us to be happy at our workplace and He stands ready to assist us in whatever we need from Him. Remember the Lord commanded Adam to dress the garden. Your workplace can be anywhere God has opened a door. For many women, the workplace is in the home. If this is the case, the rules still apply –He expects our best!

Some of the toughest times in my life were when I was unemployed. The depression would rest on my shoulders so heavily I didn't know how I would make it to the next week. Bills would start to be due and there would be no relief in sight. It seemed no matter how much I went to church and tried to give Him praise the thoughts of failure and abandonment persisted.

The enemy of my soul took every opportunity to try and crush my faith in God. It seemed with every day came new ways and reasons to give up on the Lord and all He had promised me. Though I was often ashamed and mentally fatigued, I still held on to my faith in Jesus Christ and what the Bible had promised me. I knew things would be fine if I could just make it to the next day.

I remember being embarrassed to get around people with good jobs because I would most likely be asked how my job was going, and then I would have the unfortunate opportunity to explain my misfortune. The devil would try to get me to resent anyone with a great job and spread pessimism to everyone I could concerning job security.

Chapter 5: Man's Duties In The Garden

Faith is a huge subject with many tentacles touching every avenue of our lives. Faith is not limited to the few hours we spend in church, nor any other segment of our life; our faith must be applied throughout the whole day over the course of the whole week. We must apply our Faith to our employment. What a resource to not only provide a living for ourselves, but provide a conduit to share our Faith each and every day.

Beloved, what has God commanded you to do? Perhaps I should ask what has He called you to do? If you feel alienated from God, and you are unhappy with your life as far as your work goes, perhaps you are not in the perfect will of God concerning your work. You may be in His permissible will, but not His perfect will. Remember this statement the rest of your life, "If God calls, He equips."

I do want to clarify a point. There are times in people's lives they must study for the work ahead. God understands, and even appreciates your commitment to study. For those who are involved in school, it is your work. We have to study our vocation if we are going to be good at it. Remember, God expects our best, so any attempt to short yourself out of learning to be the best may jeopardize your study, your future, and diminish your good character.

We need to be careful not to judge the calling of others if what they are doing seems to be absent of work. I never said work had to be miserable, nor did I state you had to punch a time card for God to use you. The point is, WORK! Move forward, never settle for complacency when there is so much that God expects out of us.

One of the greatest jobs available today is mocked by liberals and looked down on by many of our friends. I personally think my wife has one of the greatest jobs in the whole world, yet many would say she is lazy because of the company she chose to go to work for. On April 20, 2000 my wife received full-time employment by an institution called the HOME. Her employer was a little infant who would place some of the hardest demands on her life. Her work hours went from 40 hours a week to 168 hours, without vacation, time and a half pay, comp time and sick leave—you thought you needed a Union!

The benefit package was so good that it overcame every negative issue. The benefits package included never having to clock-out and leave her child. Darlene would most likely be present for the first smile to grace the face of a precious newborn. She would get to hear the first words spoken; see the first roll-over, crawl, and then steps. She would hear the first words joined together and formed into an innocent statement such as "love you" or "bye-bye".

Sadly, many people would call my wife, as well as millions and millions of other women, a "lazy-bum". I remember hearing people ask my wife when she was talking about staying at home with the children, "What are you going to do all day?" A remark of that sorts reveals pure ignorance. What are you going to do all day? Please, that question speaks volumes and reveals so much about the person making such an inquiry.

Yes, it is a job, but it is more than that, it is a calling. In fact, all mothers are called and directed by scripture to attend to their children. For the next decade and more Darlene will be employed in a great work place. The call of God will reconfirm her good choice throughout the days and years to come.

Let me inject this statement before moving on. There are many wonderful people who cannot stay at home with their children because of the overwhelming financial responsibilities they may be faced with. Perhaps many are all alone because of a father that walked out on them to chase after other interests instead of the responsibilities he committed himself to. If this is your case, my heart goes out to you in this situation. The Lord knows that there are many of you out there, and perhaps you dream for the day to stay home with your child.

My advice would be to find a good church to be involved in where you can make friends and have a positive male influence in the lives of your children. Perhaps many would have close family that could assist as well – take advantage of these opportunities. God hasn't abandoned you at all. If you are sacrificing, and it is to raise your children, then God will reward you in the years to come. I further believe if you are doing all you can do and have God as center stage in your life, He will restore the years of pain and frustration with years of great joy and abundance.

The Lord commanded Adam to dress the garden and He supplied his needs; it wasn't until Adam stepped away from God and deliberately sinned against Him that all his trouble started. Once again, the Lord will supply our needs as well as He supplied Adam's. We need only to believe how faithful He is. When it comes to work, God is there to fight for us. If we face layoffs, we must continue in our faith; not start, but continue to trust the Lord.

Our biggest problem as humans is that we ignore the tell-tale signs until it is too late. We take things for granted instead of discerning what is ahead. It

Chapter 5: Man's Duties In The Garden

isn't that we are not taking thought for tomorrow as the Bible commands; we are just poorly taking God-given responsibility. If you are in need of work, the Lord is there to give you peace and to supply your need. How do I know this? The concept is fundamental to God and our created purpose.

I want to reiterate a point I made earlier about unemployment and the effect it made in my life. I remember it was an awful experience. I remember that unemployment not only affected my wallet, it affected me spiritually as well. I can say it was that divine drive to work that was attacked during unemployment. I remembered trusting, that despite any opposition, God would come through. My faith was steadfast, I did not have to go and pray and get psyched up for a move of God. However, I must confess that I did solicit prayers during those dreadful times of unemployment. Through it all, God was there for me to lean on and He is there for you as well.

I remember feeling so abandoned as I searched for employment. It seemed that government sponsored job services were a mere joke in my situation, after all, who needed a preacher? A minister was the only thing I was fully qualified for except for a Taxidermist. I was good at preserving the living and the dead as well. There were no job offers in either of these areas.

Then I had to deal with the demand to work weekends and various shifts involving times that I would be ministering in church. I wasn't about to work on Sunday no matter what the cost. I knew God would grant me one favor, and that was to have Sundays off for church. I never doubted He would answer this prayer. I trusted in Him completely despite the overwhelming odds against me, but I remembered my faith went beyond the natural. My faith was moved into the fourth dimension - the spirit world. I bound every lying spirit that came against me saying that I would never find a job without working on what I declared, "The Lord's Day."

I knew in my heart that I could never really give an employer all of my attention and loyalty, because by being called to be a minister, I knew that I had to keep the doors open. I even turned down great jobs because of my determination to stay focused on ministry even though I had bills to pay. God honored my desires as well as my faith.

My particular situation was a lot different from most, I agree, but my determination to keep priorities in order was not. I never lost sight of my spiritual devotion and faith to trust God no matter what was happening around me. You see, I determined that I would stand tall and not give in to pressure - it was hard, very hard. Depression, frustration and resentment were always options readily available for the taking, but I came against the author of such wickedness. I can remember on many occasions how I would breakdown and literally cry before the Lord, but I made it and you will too.

Beloved, determined faith was the key to getting through that ordeal. Secondly, it was loved ones who stood with me, but primarily, it was the fact that I didn't have to go looking for God when bills started stacking. I didn't have to buddy up to the Lord to USE Him! God was there in a very special way. I managed to reach out to him just as I have for many years and APPLY DAILY FAITH. The financial obligations were met.

Just for the record, I want to make one thing clear. I have personally made a commitment to God that I would never work on Sunday (except for ministry obligations). This commitment is personal and as you might tell, I am committed to upholding it; however, a commitment I made to the Lord is not one which I would try and push on any reader. All days are equally important to God, all are Holy.

I feel as though I must tell you of a situation that happened in my life during such a time that I was without work. Moving on from this topic without sharing this incredible story would be unfair to you, the reader. During a time that I was job hunting, I answered an ad in a local paper for help wanted. When I called, I left a message on a recorder and for two weeks I didn't hear from this company. Frankly, I soon forgot about even applying for the job.

Then one night, two weeks later around 8:00, I received a phone call concerning the ad I had answered. After answering and asking a few questions of my own, the man on the phone wanted to meet with me the next day at a fast food restaurant thirty minutes away. I agreed, and the next day we met. After a very impersonal outdoors interview the men that met me there were impressed and said they would get up with me later in the week about starting to work.

Later that evening my wife and I had gone to bed unusually early. I was already in bed when I received a phone call almost on the hour of 10:00, from the man that had initially called me and set up the interview. The gentleman wanted me to be ready to work 3:00AM the next (Sunday) morning. My prayers were answered! This job would have paid more than I have ever made in my life and would have placed me in an income that many will never see in a lifetime.

Chapter 5: Man's Duties In The Garden

There was one major problem with accepting the job - it would require total dedication and at the time, I had a small church to pastor. If I was going to be faithful to my church, how could I dedicate myself to a job that needed me on Sundays? I really needed the work. The pay at the church wasn't enough to even pay the bills, and all of it was donations with the exception of a few that actually tithed. Yes, I had to meet my financial obligations and make a way for my wife and me. If I could not accomplish this task, I was worse than an infidel.

> *But if any provide not for his own, and specially for those of his own house, he hath denied the faith, and is worse than an infidel. (1 Timothy 5:8)*

I remember getting off the phone very excited and all of a sudden it hit me that I couldn't accept the job. This was no "could have been" opportunity; I was to start work in five hours. After discussing the job with my wife, we knew what had to be done. There was no need for discussion as far as priorities. It was hard watching the opportunity float away, but we knew we were to stand firm on our faith. Unfortunately, I didn't even have a call back number without using "*69".

The real issue at stake was FAITH. I knew that God was faithful, and He knew that I needed a job to be able to meet financial responsibilities. It was a fact of standing on the faith that I not only had, but that which I had taught for years in ministry. Friend, God knows your needs. You have only to release your burden to Him, not harbor emotions of despair and anxiety. Let the Lord take the responsibility of doing what you cannot do.

Remember, man's first responsibility was to work. Adam's job may have involved farming, but what is your responsibility? What responsibility has God delegated out to you? If you are struggling in this area, please allow the Lord to move on your behalf; don't make rash decisions that will slow down the hand of God.

Please don't ever put a job opportunity over the Lord's work if you are sure of a special calling; you will regret it for the rest of your life. I have had so many people confess that they ran from God and never had a decent week of peace in their heart until they stopped running. I am not talking about running from God's call to salvation; I am talking about running from God and His purpose for your life. Remember that God doesn't get pleasure out of watching His children go through misery. So, if God has moved on your heart, then you should move on your feet to accept His calling.

Today is the day to say, "Yes, Lord, where you lead me I will follow." As you move out and let go of what seems like security in your life, God will encompass you with a peace that passeth all understanding. Accepting the work that God has for you, even if it means keeping your present job or turning in a notice, will come naturally as you begin to move in faith. Remember, the things of God are spiritual, and therefore, they are received in faith and followed through faithfully; running will only bring more pain and confusion to your life.

Man's Second Responsibility

Man's second responsibility was to keep the garden. Remember that the Word specifically commanded man to dress and keep the Garden of Eden. At this point the command to keep the garden may go unnoticed by many, but upon close examination of the word, there is something suspicious about the language. Why would God need for man to keep the garden? Perhaps a better question would be, keep it from what, or from whom?

The word "keep" in the Hebrew means to hedge about. To hedge about as in guarding, protecting, attending. Hence there was something in the garden that Adam was supposed to protect, or guard against. Why would God create a perfect garden and then put Adam in charge of protecting it, especially when he was the first of human creation on earth. Unfortunately, we know he failed to keep the Garden, thus disobeying God's Word.

Surprisingly, this passage presents the first reference to an enemy of both God and man. Now I don't want to beat up on Adam, but it must go on record that he was warned by God of possible intrusion. All the things God may have spoken to Adam aren't recorded in the Bible. We have no idea of what Adam and God discussed in the cool of the day. I can only conclude that they just didn't sit and stare at one another every day – especially since God doesn't waste time and I am sure He had plenty to do elsewhere.

I don't have a clue concerning the ins and outs of what took place early on in the garden, but according to scripture, there is Biblical evidence to hang Adam with the crime of disobeying God. Adam failed to do his job. Of all the privileges that were granted to the first couple in the garden, God made three separate demands on them, (1) Dress and keep the Garden (2) Be fruitful, multiply, replenish, subdue and have dominion over all the earth (3) Don't eat that which is forbidden.

The Lord knew that Satan would soon show up on the scene, therefore causing problems with His new creation - man. The Lord had previously thrown him out of the heavenly host along with one third of the angels. The crime was pride, and there was nothing more tempting to Satan than to see God's creation crumble. Like Satan and all the other created beings of God, the Lord gave man a free will. Man could choose for himself what decisions to make. Though God was faithful and apparently visited with man each day, man still had the ability to choose.

Sadly, many people think that if you are a Christian you have no responsibilities, just live every day like it was your last...eat, drink, and be merry. But with being a part of God's creation, comes responsibility. God gave man the ability to be responsible because He was created in the image and the likeness of God. The Lord gives us the ability to choose, as well as the capacity to rationalize. He always allows us the freedom to decide our future, our actions, and our intentions. God wants us to serve Him because we love Him and have determined to put Him first in our lives. God receives no glory from a system that is robotic and without decision.

The Responsibility Factor

Divine responsibility works two ways. Man is responsible to God. God is responsible to man. Our free will determines where we focus our responsibility. Will we decide that we can be like Adam and disobey God and His commandment and risk the consequences? Should we allow ourselves to be out talked by a serpent and choose to believe a third party for the truth over our Creator, or should we stand firm on God's Word despite the enemy's useless lying rhetoric?

By Adam disobeying God and sinning in the garden, God had a responsibility to His Word to fulfill, and that was to carry out His judgment against humanity (Genesis 2:17). We are His creation, but because He is holy, we must face our sentence. If man would have conducted himself in the garden like he was commanded, he would have protected that which was at risk. Adam's fate depended on his ability to protect himself, and his wife, from that which was alien to the Garden.

Unfortunately, God has given us the same commandment He gave Adam thousands of years ago. God has given us the responsibility to, and, may I add, the equipment for, protecting ourselves from the attacks of our enemy (Ephesians 6:10-18). God has also given us His Word filled with instruction on how to conduct our lives. There is never an excuse to sin or give in to Satan. More so than ever we are left without any excuse - having received both Testaments as well as the Holy Spirit into our lives to direct us.

Beloved, through time and much heartache God has continued to give man the ability to protect that which was given him. We have the ability to fight and wage war against all wickedness that would seek to devour what is holy and righteous. Will we assume our responsibility, or neglect it as many choose to do? The decision is ours to make, but the consequences of our lack of responsibility will be our own fault in the end. You see, God has made a way for us to face all our problems, even a way of escape from all temptation (1 Corinthians. 10:13).

If we choose to protect what is ours and guard ourselves against all temptation of the evil one, we too can live an abundant life in Christ. The focus is our need to practice Adam's command in the garden, not look back and ask absurd questions. We have the chance and ability, which the power of the blood of Jesus Christ afforded us through Salvation, to stake our ground and refuse to give in to the subtle attacks of Satan. Consider the scripture below.

Ye are of God, little children, and have overcome them: because greater is he (God) that is in you, than he (Devil) that is in the world. (1 John 4:4)

Our defense is one that should be constant, structured, and Christ centered. When we come to the point we say to ourselves I have to stand and not keep giving in, the battle is half won. It is not too late to prepare to defend, but know this my friend, each time you give in and lose ground, you lose something. I know we lose precious non-redeemable time. As far as other losses, we may never know. You can be assured of this one thing, we suffer loss, and that loss, though it may be recovered, was a loss all the same. It will take some action that is time consuming to overcome that which was lost.

Beloved, think about this fact; Adam gave in once; look at the price he had to pay. Better than that, look at the price you and I have had to pay – for his sin! I wonder how much his second sin set him back. Friend, how is sin setting you back? What price are you paying for your sins? The real key is applying faith every day to live out the will of God in your life. It's not the big decisions in front of a congregation, or the keeping of a big promise that make a difference in our lives. What will make the difference is simply walking an obedient faith filled life every day before both God and man.

Our obedience starts now, not later, because like dieting, an obedient life has to start now. If we delay, we will pay. The fruits of a faith filled life can

Chapter 5: Man's Duties In The Garden

begin immediately if we simply start to move toward fulfilling God's will in our lives. Those faithful brothers and sisters we often look up to didn't get where they are by procrastinating in the faith. They made a sound decision to commit their life to fulfilling God's plan in and through their life. From our viewpoint they come across as super heroes of faith; however, they know they were willing servants of the faith, facing the same battles as you and I.

The real difference will come with everyday practical Christian living coming through the constant application of your faith. Those little decisions, those little nos to the devil, add up in a big way. We live in a generation of big things, big decisions, big houses, big cars, and big money; it is the little things that truly matter in this life, such as doing what God demands of us the first time, all the time, not part or most of the time. Too many times we focus on the big things instead of being faithful in the little things. While any deviation from righteousness makes a difference and is certainly looked upon as sin by our Holy Father, we are warned that the little foxes spoil the vine.

My friend, God told Adam to dress and keep the garden, not too much to ask. God is making demands on your life as well. You and you alone know those commands. Only you will have to give an account for the actions you have taken. Whether they were right or wrong, God will call on you to give an account. Will you submit to those demands and give God full authority in your life, or will you fail to do that which is required just as Adam did? Will you open your heart and let the light of God's Word and the power of the Holy Spirit flow through you and search out and cleanse all the impurities?

Let me share a secret with you. Please never forget the point I am about to make. Our enemy provokes us in this "Big World" with little decisions that confront our faith. Sure, we have those big opportunities to really mess up our lives, but it is those little ones that hang us. In chapter two of Song of Solomon, verse fifteen Solomon writes, *"Take us the foxes, the little foxes, that spoil the vines: for our vines have tender grapes."* Solomon wanted to catch those little foxes because they caused the real damage to the vineyard, not the big foxes.

The Word is telling us it is those opportunities we take to dishonestly cover ourselves by insinuating something other than the truth, such as making a promise and breaking it, gossiping about someone when we have no right to, stealing from our employer by wasting valuable time on the job. These little things really hurt us as badly as the things we perceive as big. Sin is sin in the eyes of our Lord, whether it is not returning the extra few cents of change the cashier overpaid us, or breaking the speed limits, it doesn't matter to a Holy Righteous God.

Many Christians subconsciously categorize sin. People have various imaginations of a scale stretching from one extreme to the next. On one end of the scale we have those cardinal sins, such as murder, rape, homosexuality, then up the scale we have adultery, "you know everybody is doing it," then maybe one night stands with the single folks, or frequent fornication with our girlfriends or boyfriends. Further up the scale you may have the lying and cheating.

Toward the end of the scale the murky gray area kicks in. We find ourselves approaching the "so-called" disputable sins of man. Then right on the tip end we see breaking speed limits, littering, wasting time on the job, overeating and maybe "informative gossip." Yes, we have our own little slide-rule to measure sin as we see it through our own understanding.

Some of these sins are little to us, but they are inexcusable to God. I know, I know, it is those hideous acts of violence such as murder, rape, and battery that really make the difference… wrong. This is the rationale the Devil would like us to believe. How unfortunate that this trickle-down morality has whitewashed sin so much the above mentioned is about all many churchgoers consider a real offence to God.

Sin is sin! All sin is the same. From the violent and hideous acts of Adolf Hitler to the teenager who deliberately walks out of a convenience store with stolen candy, it is all the same to God. My friend, righteousness is righteousness. What is holy is pure and untainted with any sin. There are no scales of righteousness. We live in a black and white world when it comes to the holiness of God. The church has not been given a right in the twenty first century to make rulings on what is to be considered a sin or not. Abortion, despite any court findings or legislation, will always be an aggressive, hideous, brutal, sadistic act of murder toward a precious innocent child of God.

To protect ourselves from the enemy, we must tune in to the Holy Spirit and listen to the Lord instead of reasoning with the devil. It is an everyday struggle, but God gives us strength to war against the enemy. We must protect our heart. We must protect ourselves from the forces of evil about us. We must learn how to say no to evil and to our flesh.

Is this an easy process? Absolutely not! But it is one we can eventually win through the power of the Holy Spirit flowing in our lives. Once again, we

Chapter 5: Man's Duties In The Garden

must always understand no matter how things seem, or how bad things get, we will not be the only ones to have ever gone through the crises we face. Remember this; the mind is always at battle in the war of the flesh. Even Paul the Apostle understood the power of the flesh. He understood the constant fight that goes on within ourselves, or as he put it, our members.

Listen to the way Paul describes his fight against the carnal nature warring against him. Listen to the emotion of this passage as Paul so wonderfully describes the hideous battle we all are enlisted in.

> *For we know that the law is spiritual: but I am carnal, sold under sin. For that which I do I allow not: for what I would, that do I not; but what I hate, that do I. If then I do that which I would not, I consent unto the law that it is good. Now then it is no more I that do it, but sin that dwelleth in me. For I know that in me (that is, in my flesh,) dwelleth no good thing: for to will is present with me; but how to perform that which is good I find not. For the good that I would I do not: but the evil which I would not, that I do. Now if I do that I would not, it is no more I that do it, but sin that dwelleth in me. I find then a law, that, when I would do good, evil is present with me. For I delight in the law of God after the inward man: But I see another law in my members, warring against the law of my mind, and bringing me into captivity to the law of sin which is in my members. O wretched man that I am! who shall deliver me from the body of this death? I thank God through Jesus Christ our Lord. So then with the mind I myself serve the law of God; but with the flesh the law of sin. (Romans 7: 14-25)*

How do we protect ourselves? First and foremost, we need to protect ourselves from our destiny. Apart from God we have all been cursed, and because of the sin curse, we have all been sentenced to die and spend eternity in hell. *"But the fearful, and unbelieving, and the abominable, and murderers, and whoremongers, and sorcerers, and idolaters, and all liars, shall have their part in the lake which burneth with fire and brimstone: which is the second death. (Revelations 21:8)"* By the way, that includes you and me and all our sins as well.

Next, we need to avoid the very appearance of evil.

Abstain from all appearance of evil. (1 Thessalonians 5:22)

We may avoid the appearance of evil by censoring what comes through our eyes, ears, touch, and even mouth. We also can avoid evil by watching what comes out of our mouth as well. With a careful eye we can look into Proverbs and understand the use, or misuse of the tongue.

> *Thou art snared with the words of thy mouth, thou art taken with the words of thy mouth. (Proverbs 6:2)*
>
> *The heart of the wise teacheth his mouth, and addeth learning to his lips. (Proverbs 16:23)*
>
> *Whoso keepeth his mouth and his tongue keepeth his soul from troubles. (Proverbs 21:23)*

I want you to notice what happened after God had to judge Adam and Eve for their behavior in the garden. God told Adam to dress the garden. In other words, till it, make sure the soil was loose around the vegetables, fruit, and herbs. What was once easy, maybe a bit time consuming, the Lord cursed and made it a rigorous, laborious, back-breaking task. Weeds were to take over and man would have to work by the sweat of his brow to manage food. Where great food once grew freely with man's help in cultivating the soil, weeds would now choke and bind up the ground.

Because man failed to keep the garden and protect it from the devil, God set this earth on a course and turned its authority over to the devil making him the pseudo-ruler of this world. My point is this - if you don't protect what God has given, you will lose it or suffer dreadful consequences. Let us look to the Word of God in these two passages of scripture:

> *In whom the god of this world hath blinded the minds of them which believe not, lest the light of the glorious gospel of Christ, who is the image of God, should shine unto them. (2 Corinthians 4:4)*
>
> *Wherein in time past ye walked according to the course of this world, according to the prince of the power of the air, the spirit that now worketh in the children of disobedience: (Ephesians 2:2)*

As we can clearly see according to the Word of God, Adam's sin certainly changed the earth around us, and even the authority structure was turned over for a time. I believe the picture is clear for each of us. If you want to trust God for the power to help you take control of your responsibilities, He is ready. God is not only ready to help you meet your responsibilities, but He will delightfully keep His as well.

Good faith is bigger than the Word itself. To have faith in anything else but our Lord is absolutely reckless as well as futile. Today we have been bombarded with so much teaching on faith that one may assume God will give us anything we trust in. Sadly, so many have been trusting in things that the heart of God is a million miles from.

God's word is adamant. We have two things to do, work, and keep our home from anything that would come against it. The two must be used in balance. If we continue to work, the devil will creep in and destroy our home. Such truth is clear when you consider those who spend so much time away from their home at work. Later we find the house, spouse, and children have gone to rot.

On the other side, if we continue to watch and regard not the work that needs to be done, our families will starve, and then, according to the Word we are worse off than an infidel. When we apply our faith, God stands ready to assist us with supernatural power to accomplish His will while we are fulfilling our responsibilities.

God is ready to put the past behind and put you back where you belong. Seek the Lord's guidance and call on Him to help you establish that healthy balance of work and responsibility. The Lord is ready for you to apply faith and remain committed from this point forward in your walk with Him. Are you ready to accept responsibility and determined to live faithful for God from this day on? If you answered yes, and especially if you are struggling in the previously discussed areas, let us pray.

Prayer:

Dear Lord, I thank You for the authority of the blood of Jesus Christ my Savior. I ask You to forgive me for not taking control of my responsibilities as a Christian. I confess to You I have failed and I am seeking Your guidance from this point on. I realize I can do nothing without Your help. I also confirm I want to live my life according to Your will, not mine. Lord help me be able to stand against the wiles of the devil and be the person you intended me to be. I ask You to lead me by Your Holy Spirit and help me be submissive and discerning of Your ways.

Lord, help me protect my heart against all evil. Help me to shield myself in every possible way from what is wicked, while committing myself to the things You have called me to do. Lord, help me to understand Your Word with wisdom and knowledge, that I may glorify Thy kingdom in all I do on this earth. Forgive me where I have failed, and heal the error of my previous ways. I ask these things in Jesus' Name, Amen.

6 | Who Is In Control Of The Earth?

And you hath he quickened, who were dead in trespasses and sins: Wherein in time past ye walked according to the course of this world, according to the prince of the power of the air, the spirit that now worketh in the children of disobedience: (Ephesians 2:1-2)

What about the course of this world? Is it possible this earth is on a course? We see according to this passage mankind is walking according to a course, and the course is that which the children of disobedience walk in. When Paul was writing to the Ephesians, what kind of point was he really trying to make in reference to a course?

One of the most interesting facts Christians wrestle with is the course of this world, and the one who is presently in control of our planet. Everything is getting worse. Morally man is descending into the depths of the abyss. Hell is enlarging itself. My friends, life is tougher, sin is more open, violence is increasing, crime is taking over our little neighborhoods. Why? Satan is in charge of this earth. He is the Prince of this world. Fact is, all you have to do is read the back of the Bible.

Many faith teachers find these facts rather insulting to their high glamour faith teachings, choosing to ignore and/or deny the obvious facts set before them. Often such teachers find themselves theologically painted in a corner. Questions about recent unexplained occurrences in the world and particularly a Christian's life, find such so-called teachers dumbfounded. Often they will resort to memorized rhetoric that, more often than not, is

Chapter 6: Who Is In Control Of The Earth?

third party to the Bible, and completely unsupported by scripture or taken way out of context.

The approach to understanding this earth and the power struggle is key to drawing strength and faith for the Christian. Facts regarding the supernatural controlling elements, or should we say powers of this earth, are sometimes shocking to most, often resented by others, and unbelievable to many. The pain of admitting things are not getting better because of the course we are on causes many to avoid real scriptural debate.

Just who is in control of the earth? Ultimately, God, but for the present, Satan (has been given) is in control of not only the earth, but also the whole universe. Wow! Imagine Satan being in control of the universe as we know it. Yes that statement may sound a little blasphemous, but it is the hard truth as backed by scripture.

Now, let us be honest and practical for one moment. Can you say all the mess in which we are finding ourselves is God's work? Does it really appear God is in control of our communities, our schools, our entertainment industry and etc.? Now don't get all theological on me yet, just put on your seat belt and hang in there for a moment. I know everybody likes to get all fuzzy when it comes to grand plans of Christians taking back over and revival coming to America, but let us be soberly honest with one another.

I once heard a preacher tell how one minister explained how things were slowly getting better, and how Christians were slowly getting a foothold in politics and so forth. The listening minister posed one question that ransacked the others theology, "Do you have less locks on your door than you did twenty years ago?"

A point well made. Are things getting better? No. Life is more demanding than ever. Crime is rising even in predominantly safe neighborhoods in America. Honestly, for someone to take the local newspaper and assert that abuse, crime, and poverty is diminishing - they are either mentally out of touch, grossly blind to all truth, or lying to themselves and others.

Oh, there will always be those who live in a detached social arena separated from the rest of us, protected by the wealth of this world, living inside compounds, and therefore, not having any/or limited contact with others. They will probably see things as going really well in their circle of power. Unfortunately, only a small fraction of society has the wherewithal to live in that kind of world. As for you and me, we live in reality.

Of course there are always those generational politicians who have fed off our tax money, having never really grasped the idea of the real world outside their aristocratic clique. They wouldn't be familiar with wondering where their next meal would come from, or if they would be able to pay rent on time. These elitists often have a warped view of this world, thinking everything is getting better with the growth of big government.

They think the school system will fix itself with more spending, more taxes, and let us not forget the lottery --You know, "it's for the children." Strangely, the vast majority of politicians send their children to private schools because they want a quality education and a safe environment for their little Johnny. If the world is getting better, then why don't they become part of it instead of hiding in exclusive suburban private neighborhoods?

Over the past years of ministry, I have encountered some people pretty naive to their surroundings. I must admit, after being raised in a small rural segregated community in southern Alabama, I had no concept of life across the two rivers separating us from the rest of the world. In fact after becoming an adult I remember being overwhelmed finding out some of the things that were commonplace to everyone else.

In the little community where I was born and raised we didn't have any crime to speak of. About the most exciting thing around my house was election night in the hunting club and catching night hunters. When I grew up and got a driver's license, I discovered a whole new civilization across the rivers, one that was full of wickedness.

Simply put, Satan is the ruler of this earth. He has this earth on a crash course. Everything that is not directly controlled by Christians is controlled by the devil. While God is ultimately in control, the rights to earth have been given over to Satan because of man's rebellion through sin. The devil is full of hate and has no mercy on what is righteous. He hates God, and he will hate you if you are a blood-bought child of God. *John 10:10 "The thief cometh not, but for to steal, and to kill, and to destroy: I am come that they might have life, and that they might have it more abundantly."*

Notice how Jesus refers to Satan in these three passages from John's Gospel

> *Now is the judgment of this world: now shall the prince of this world be cast out. (John 12:31)*

> *Hereafter I will not talk much with you: for the prince of this world cometh, and hath nothing in me. (John 14:30)*
>
> *Of judgment, because the prince of this world is judged. (John 16:11)*

When we look at the names of Satan found in the Bible, we can clearly get a good perspective of his own power, devious deeds, and character. Here is an "AKA" list of the names found in the Bible that Satan is called:

Accuser of the Brethren
Adversary
Angel of Light
Beelzebub
Belial
Devil
Dragon
Enemy
God of this World
King over all the Children of Pride
Leviathan
Lucifer
Prince of Devils
Prince of the Power of the Air
Prince of this World
Satan
Serpent
Tempter
The Anointed Cherub
The Thief
Wicked One

Taking Authority over the Devil

No matter how ugly Satan is, and as powerful as he may seem, he is under the authority of God, and therefore, fully under our authority as scripture teaches. Though Satan has control over this world, we have been given authority over him if we are children of God. We have this assurance given to us by the Word of God.

> *And He said unto them, "Go ye into all the world, and preach the gospel to every creature. He that believeth and is baptized shall be saved; but he that believeth not shall be damned. And these signs shall follow*

them that believe; In My name shall they cast out devils; they shall speak with new tongues; they shall take up serpents; and if they drink any deadly thing, it shall not hurt them; they shall lay hands on the sick, and they shall recover". (Mark 16: 15-18)

I have written unto you, fathers, because ye have known Him that is from the beginning. I have written unto you, young men, because ye are strong, and the word of God abideth in you, and ye have overcome the wicked one. Love not the world, neither the things that are in the world. If any man love the world, the love of the Father is not in him. For all that is in the world, the lust of the flesh, and the lust of the eyes, and the pride of life, is not of the Father, but is of the world. And the world passeth away, and the lust thereof: but he that doeth the will of God abideth forever. (1 John 2: 14-17)

As children of God we have the power available to us to overcome Satan by the Word of God. Just as Jesus defeated Satan in the desert by standing on the written Word, we too have authority given to us; however, we must accept this authority. If we do not accept this authority, Satan will hit us wide open in hopes of destroying our faith. He will blind-side us when we least expect it, and try to shipwreck our faith. We will be vigilant as we apply our faith on a daily basis, by staying in God's Word and constantly praying.

When we feel our back is against the wall, we must simply apply our faith. When there seems to be no hope for tomorrow, we simply must stand on the precious promises of God. Remember, we have dominion over every power in Hell. While we should never forget who is in control of this world, we must remember that He in whom we have our faith overcame death, hell, and the grave (*Revelations 1:18*).

The simple point here is to understand this earth has nothing to offer you and me. Do not put your faith in this world. Do not lay up treasure upon this earth. If you are a Christian, this earth and its wicked dwellers will hate you and all you stand for. Remember, we are simply pilgrims passing through (*1 Peter 2:11*). We must apply all our faith toward things that are eternal, not the things of this world. The Bible is very clear concerning how things will perish in the last days.

You see beloved, not only is it important to apply your faith, but it is equally important to know where to apply it. Let's consider the scripture below to bring further insight.

Chapter 6: Who Is In Control Of The Earth?

> *Lay not up for yourselves treasures upon earth, where moth and rust doth corrupt, and where thieves break through and steal: but lay up for yourselves treasures in heaven, where neither moth nor rust doth corrupt, and where thieves do not break through nor steal. (Matthew 6:19-20)*
>
> *But seek ye first the kingdom of God, and His righteousness; and all these things shall be added unto you. (Matthew 6:33)*

Beloved, all we do, let us do for the Kingdom of God. Let us put our efforts toward accomplishing that over which we have been given power. Too many times Christians get caught up in this world and all its tricks and gimmicks. This so-called prosperity gospel is a counterfeit; therefore, much of it is lies. Scripture teaches that everything we can touch, see, smell, taste, and hear will be burned over; only those things we cannot see will remain (2 Peter 3:10).

All the gold on this earth cannot compare to the gold we shall tread upon in heaven. On earth man will kill for a chunk of gold no larger than a field-pea, and one day, we shall enter in through gates of pearl, walls of jasper, and walk on streets of gold. Our focus should be laying up treasure in heaven, laboring as a witness to the lost, and supporting those in need. Instead of investing all our time and money in the stock market, we should certainly diversify our portfolio to include some futures – in heaven that is!

In the final analysis of scripture presented in this chapter, I think it would be wise for one to apply his or her faith in areas that do not involve investing in earth or earthly goods. No one in their right mind would invest in a company they knew was going to lose every bit of its value and assets overnight. Concerning spiritual things, we should invest just as carefully as we would in the stock market.

In conclusion I must pose this sobering question: Why, then, do we allow so much energy to be spent on the things that will fade away or burn in the end? We shouldn't waste our faith to see it put to a test and lose because we placed our bid on a bad horse. Apply your faith in an area we have assurance in, such as the coming Kingdom of God, and anything else God seeks for our life. We know our enemy, we know his authority, we know the fate of this earth; therefore, it is high time we go with a winning team when it comes to applying faith.

Application of our faith in any direction that does not move us closer to our Lord, strengthen our faith and the faith of others, and fulfill God's will in our life is poor stewardship of time and human resources. Once again, we know the fate of this world; we need to build on those things that are eternal, or things that put us in a better situation to make an eternal difference in ourselves and others around us.

> *For all things are for your sakes, that the abundant grace might through the thanksgiving of many redound to the glory of God. For which cause we faint not; but though our outward man perish, yet the inward man is renewed day by day. For our light affliction, which is but for a moment, worketh for us a far more exceeding and eternal weight of glory; While we look not at the things which are seen, but at the things which are not seen: for the things which are seen are temporal; but the things which are not seen are eternal. (1Corinthians 4: 15-18)*

Prayer:

Lord, help me realize in Whom I shall put my faith. Help me realize at all times who my enemy is. Give me insight and understanding concerning the things of this world and their constant appeal to my flesh. Help me discern what is purposeful and conducive to living a faithful life separated unto You, my Lord. Give me the faith I need to walk according to Your will and abstain from getting caught up in my own. Help me to remember I am merely a pilgrim passing through this world, headed for a city which hath foundations, whose builder and maker is You. Last of all, give me wisdom to labor in the faith, putting all foolish worldly desires (that will pass away) to the side, choosing to labor in those things which are perfect and eternal. Amen.

7 | The Effects Of Man's Sin In The Garden

What was the effect of sin on mankind? After man had sinned in the garden, what changes would forever shape the destiny of civilization? Many have asked these and other very sobering questions concerning the fall of man. The Bible gives plenty of answers to these and other questions regarding our subject.

One of the greatest effects of mans' fall was that he lost his God given ability to lead in a totalitarian planetary system. Based on scripture, Adam had a wonderful, and I believe, very different relationship with the Lord. What is interesting is no one knows the amount of time they spent together before Adam's sin. Adam and Eve could have lived for a long time before the serpent showed up to tempt man. It is my understanding many scholars believe man sinned shortly after his creation. No one really knows, so one opinion is a good as another.

The facts are, not only did man commune with God, but there were some other differences as well. The animal kingdom was not frightened of man, nor was man frightened of it. The plant kingdom was the sole provider of food. In short, man and beast were to be vegetarians in the garden. Consider the passage below. God creates a menu for every living being, including man.

> And God said, "Behold, I have given you every herb bearing seed, which is upon the face of all the earth, and every tree, in the which is the fruit of a tree yielding seed; to you it shall be for meat. And to every beast of the earth, and to every fowl of the air, and to every thing that creepeth

Chapter 7: The Effects Of Man's Sin In The Garden

upon the earth, wherein there is life, I have given every green herb for meat:" and it was so. And God saw every thing that he had made, and, behold, it was very good. And the evening and the morning were the sixth day. (Gen 1:29-31)

My friend, it looks like Adam and Eve had it made in the garden. They had their pick of food, with one exception. Of all the trees in the garden, there was only one tree that could not be partaken of. The Lord had placed two trees in the garden that were of unique value to man, as well as concern to God. In the garden God placed a Tree of Life and the Tree of the Knowledge of Good and Evil, God told man not to eat of the Tree of the Knowledge of Good and Evil.

And the LORD God commanded the man, saying, Of every tree of the garden thou mayest freely eat: but of the Tree of the Knowledge of Good and Evil, thou shalt not eat of it: for in the day that thou eatest thereof thou shalt surely die. (Genesis 2:16-17)

Beloved, I have heard and read it said and written by medical professionals that the human body was made to live forever. Doctors really don't understand death; they just know it happens and often understand the reason for it. As for the body, they are confused because they don't understand how a body that regenerates itself dies. Perhaps the reason is in the curse of man and the removal of the Tree of Life.

Below are listed prophecies concerning the Tree of Life. Consider what the Bible has to say about this tree and the significance of it in heaven.

He that hath an ear, let him hear what the Spirit saith unto the churches; To him that overcometh will I give to eat of the Tree of Life, which is in the midst of the paradise of God. (Revelations 2:7)

And he showed me a pure river of water of life, clear as crystal, proceeding out of the throne of God and of the Lamb. In the midst of the street of it, and on either side of the river, was there the Tree of Life, which bare twelve manner of fruits, and yielded her fruit every month: and the leaves of the tree were for the healing of the nations. And there shall be no more curse: but the throne of God and of the Lamb shall be in it; and his servants shall serve him. (Revelations 22: 1-3)

Blessed are they that do His commandments, that they may have right to the Tree of Life, and may enter in through the gates into the city. 15For without are dogs, and sorcerers, and whoremongers, and

> murderers, and idolaters, and whosoever loveth and maketh a lie. (Revelations 22:14-15)

Now, the reason for the Tree of Life's removal is simple.

> And the LORD God said, "Behold, the man is become as one of Us, to know good and evil: and now, lest he put forth his hand, and take also of the Tree of Life, and eat, and live for ever:" Therefore the LORD God sent him forth from the garden of Eden, to till the ground from whence he was taken. So He drove out the man; and He placed at the east of the garden of Eden cherubims, and a flaming sword which turned every way, to keep the way of the Tree of Life. (Genesis 3:22-24)

To summarize what God was doing here is elementary. God, being just and holy, removed man from eternally living in a sinful state that God could do nothing about. Let's clarify that last statement. The Lord is sovereign to do as He wills as long as it doesn't go against His own Word which we know as the Bible. There are certain laws God put into existence; there are certain limitations as well.

The Lord gave man liberty to choose life or death. Man clearly, by his own actions, chose to die in the garden. He made a fatal decision to know right from wrong, but God intervened and withstood him from eternally living in a pitiful damned state; hence, God rescued man from sin that day.

Once man received his just reward for sin, eternal damnation, God, in His mercy, made a simple way for man to justify himself; He overcame eternal damnation through atonement. The whole process of atonement would take thousands of years to complete. That day, instead of God taking the life of man for his wicked sin, God, in His mercy, slew an animal and made clothes to cover mans' shame and received the blood as atonement for his sin. God further knew the millions of gallons of blood from animals would never be enough to completely cleanse one's sin. Our Father knew that some day He would have to offer His own Son as a final sacrifice for man's sins.

> But this Man, after He had offered one sacrifice for sins for ever, sat down on the right hand of God; (Hebrews 10:12)

Let me attempt to spiritualize the nakedness of man for a moment. Before man's sin, God was his covering. God was man's sole provider. God was man's sole protector. Man's obedience to God protected him from all harm. Without the knowledge of good and evil, man was simply living forever in a wonderful paradise. The degree of man's residence and amenities would be

Chapter 7: The Effects Of Man's Sin In The Garden

determined by his obedience to God's Word. Of course we know Man failed in obedience, lost his residence, and had to work and sweat for everything he gained from that point on.

Though Adam and Eve were naked in the flesh, they were covered on the inside. After sin, God covered man on the outside and stripped him bare on the inside. All these things transpired as a result of man's sin in the Garden. Man would never be the same again; he would now know right from wrong. Furthermore, man would rebel against all righteousness; his heart would turn dark and cold. Never again would man feel the presence of God like he felt it in the Garden of Eden.

Even to this day, man hasn't been able to regain all he lost in the Garden. Even though we can enjoy the love of God in our hearts and the move of the Holy Spirit in our lives, there are some things we will never enjoy until we are glorified. We will have trials and tribulations to go through. We will have to watch as loved ones die before our eyes. We will endure pain and suffering and see others endure as well. We will experience sickness, and for some, sickness unto death.

We will inevitably see good people suffer bad things, leaving us asking many questions. All this is a result of mans' sin in the Garden. Yes, all this is the effect of mans' sin in the Garden of Eden - what a price the world has had to pay. Remember the Bible declares, "*For the wages of sin is death...*"

My friend, we will never understand the whole story of Genesis. The hidden mysteries any student of the Word searches for will never be completely answered in our lifetime. All we know is what the Bible tells us about concerning the first accounts of man, as well as his fall. We can only speculate on some things and gather facts throughout scripture to try to answer the rest. One day we will understand a lot of things; moreover, I believe the desire to know will be removed by the presence of God and a life of glorious eternity.

I thought I would take some time to share another view of the first accounts of man. Amazingly enough, secular history supports the Bible in its account of Adam and Eve and their tragic fall in the Garden. Babylonian inscriptions have been found referring to the "Tree of Life". The account defines man as being driven away from this tree because of evil spirits possessing a serpent and using it to defile man, and cherubs now guard the tree from man. Among some of the tablets is the story of Adapa. Adapa was the Babylonian Adam- Adapa meaning "seed of mankind".

The British Museum contains what is known as the Babylonian Temptation Seal. This Seal depicts a Tree bearing fruit in the middle of the seal. On the right side is a man, on the left, a woman plucking fruit from the tree. Directly behind the woman is a serpent standing upright and seemingly behind the ear as if whispering to the woman. It doesn't even take a child's imagination to clearly see and interpret it as the account in the Garden of Eden.

Next, there is the seal found in Nineveh in 1932 by Dr. E. A. Speiser, of the University Museum of Pennsylvania. The seal dates back to around 3500 BC and depicts a man and woman walking as if heart-broken followed by a serpent.

One might wonder how the Creation and Fall of Man episode spread into all those countries. How did so many know about the creation of Adam and Eve, or an account of a serpent beguiling man? Furthermore, the facts of early man's expansion were found in recent discovered inscriptions among nations which existed prior to the Flood.

One very interesting observation is that despite Noah and his family arriving safely on Mt. Ararat, some 500 miles from where he started, in little time the Bible shifts its attention back to the region where Noah first lived. I guess the family didn't like living in modern Turkey - that is if the Ark is really located where most scholars say it is. There are a lot of mixed theories on this account. Many have come to the understanding that tradition is proving to be wrong and totally unsupported by any close examination.

According to Babylonian tradition, Noah was from the city of Fara about 70 miles from the supposed location of the Garden of Eden. The city rested on the Euphrates River where Noah was probably familiar with boat building. Babylonian inscriptions suggest river traffic and boat building were one of man's first accomplishments in what is understood as a very advanced civilization. Archaeologists have found painted pottery, tools, vases, copper mirrors, fish hooks, cosmetics, tools, farm tools, models of boats, ruins of temples painted red or plaster coated. Pottery, painted with geometric patterns and figures of birds has been found.

Certainly there must have been an accurate link between Adam, pre-flood, and post-flood civilization. Maybe the missing link is Methuselah, the oldest man that ever lived. According to the Bible, Methuselah's life overlapped Adam's by 243 years. Noah's son, Shem, was overlapped by Methuselah by

Chapter 7: The Effects Of Man's Sin In The Garden

98 years. Imagine Methuselah and Adam talking around a campfire about the golden days in the Garden of Eden.

It is easy to see how the events in the Garden might have spread when we take a close look at Noah's family. For certain his children did not hang around the Ark until they got old. Both the Bible and history provide evidence of the migration of Noah's children. Each son went his own way and started fresh, therefore changing the earth and its population forever. The earth would never be the same again after the flood, but all the great stories, myths, rumors, and superstitions would find their own place in the new and inevitable civilizations that would follow.

Noah's three sons, Japheth, Ham, and Shem, would migrate to lands never occupied by man. Theologians assert Japheth apparently went to the North and settled lands around the Black and Caspian Sea, later settling into Europe and Asia. Ham journeyed South and settled Arabia, and the coast area of Africa including Egypt. Shem's portion of land stretched from the Mediterranean Sea all the way to the Indian Ocean, entailing the land that would eventually become Palestine.

What was the toll upon mankind due to the sin in the Garden? Life was different than during those days when God visited in the cool of the day. Man paid a price that was passed down to every generation thereafter. Nearly every civilization has their story about the creation, and the fall of man, but did they really know the consequences that would follow.

After man's sin in the Garden, there were many effects which forever changed the relationship of man toward God, nature, and society at large. According to the Bible man was separated from God by his sins; this alone had the most tragic effect on mankind. Imagine God's most precious accomplishment, man, eternally being cut-off from Him. There is no wonder why God has made every available way for man to come back to Him and be reconciled.

> *But your iniquities have separated between you and your God, and your sins have hid His face from you, that He will not hear. (Isaiah 59:2)*

Along with being separated from God, man obtained an evil conscience and a deceitful heart full of corruption. Never again would man's mind be pure and free from the presence of evil. God warned man to keep the Garden, but he failed God and allowed the serpent to deceive his wife.

Let us draw near with a true heart in full assurance of faith, having our hearts sprinkled from an evil conscience, and our bodies washed with pure water. (Hebrews 10:22)

Because it entereth not into his heart, but into the belly, and goeth out into the draught, purging all meats? And He said, "That which cometh out of the man, that defileth the man. For from within, out of the heart of men, proceed evil thoughts, adulteries, fornications, murders..." (Mark 7:19-21)

Man was to become stubborn and rebellious after the fall. His mind would no longer be one which longed for a relationship with his Creator, but rather one which would rebel against all authority and reject communion with God. Sadly our sinful nature would turn us against the One who first loved us.

Ye stiffnecked and uncircumcised in heart and ears, ye do always resist the Holy Ghost: as your fathers did, so do ye. (Acts 7:51)

Because the carnal mind is enmity against God: for it is not subject to the law of God, neither indeed can be. (Romans 8:7)

Man became evil minded against the Lord. His thoughts and deeds centered on himself and every imaginable wickedness. Ungodliness prevailed against all righteousness, and soon there wasn't but one family on earth found righteous enough to save the earth. I wonder, have we too become so alienated from what is righteous that our minds continually study evil? After all, with the world in the shape it is, and every putrefied attempt to entertain and inform this godless society, I wonder how close we are to devastation?

And God saw that the wickedness of man was great in the earth, and that every imagination of the thoughts of his heart was only evil continually. (Genesis 6:5)

The fact of the matter is, when man sinned in the garden, he became a servant to sin.

Jesus answered them, "Verily, verily, I say unto you, whosoever committeth sin is the servant of sin." (John 8:34)

We have all committed sin before God. The Bible reminds us *"all have sinned and come short of the glory of God."* We, at one time or another in our lives, have been the servants of sin. Every person upon this earth has sinned before a holy God, and because we have sinned, we are dead in our sins, and without Christ in our life, we will eternally be dead.

> *And you hath He quickened, who were dead in trespasses and sins: Wherein in time past ye walked according to the course of this world, according to the prince of the power of the air, the spirit that now worketh in the children of disobedience: Among whom also we all had our conversation in times past in the lusts of our flesh, fulfilling the desires of the flesh and of the mind; and were by nature the children of wrath, even as others. But God, who is rich in mercy, for His great love wherewith He loved us, Even when we were dead in sins, hath quickened us together with Christ, (by grace ye are saved;) (Ephesians 2:1-5)*

Because of our separated relationship from God we are eternally doomed without Him. Beloved, this world has absolutely no hope outside of Jesus Christ and His atoning blood. The world teaches a brighter message, but God declares otherwise. There is no salvation within. There is no salvation in nature. The trees and precious stones of this earth cannot redeem a man from his pitiful lost state.

> *The wicked shall be turned into hell, and all the nations that forget God. (Psalms 9:17)*

> *And these shall go away into everlasting punishment: but the righteous into life eternal. (Matthew 25:46)*

Man also became victim to sickness, suffering, and even death. We are doomed and the doctors and lawyers can do nothing to restore pitiful man. Today, sickness rages all over the world. AIDS is destroying African nations. Heart disease is on the increase. Diabetes is out of control in America and now plaguing her youth. Famine is annihilating thousands of people a day in third world countries.

> *Because the creature itself also shall be delivered from the bondage of corruption into the glorious liberty of the children of God. For we know that the whole creation groaneth and travaileth in pain together until now. And not only they, but ourselves also, which have the firstfruits of the Spirit, even we ourselves groan within ourselves, waiting for the adoption, to wit, the redemption of our body. (Romans 8:21-23)*

> *And said, If thou wilt diligently hearken to the voice of the LORD thy God, and wilt do that which is right in His sight, and wilt give ear to His commandments, and keep all His statutes, I will put none of these*

diseases upon thee, which I have brought upon the Egyptians: for I am the LORD that healeth thee. (Exodus 15:26)

Not only was our relationship with God affected in all ways, but God saw fit to burden the human race with curse and hard labor.

And the LORD God said unto the serpent, Because thou hast done this, thou art cursed above all cattle, and above every beast of the field; upon thy belly shalt thou go, and dust shalt thou eat all the days of thy life: And I will put enmity between thee and the woman, and between thy seed and her seed; it shall bruise thy head, and thou shalt bruise His heel. Unto the woman he said, I will greatly multiply thy sorrow and thy conception; in sorrow thou shalt bring forth children; and thy desire shall be to thy husband, and he shall rule over thee. And unto Adam he said, Because thou hast hearkened unto the voice of thy wife, and hast eaten of the tree, of which I commanded thee, saying, Thou shalt not eat of it: cursed is the ground for thy sake; in sorrow shalt thou eat of it all the days of thy life; Thorns also and thistles shall it bring forth to thee; and thou shalt eat the herb of the field; In the sweat of thy face shalt thou eat bread, till thou return unto the ground; for out of it wast thou taken: for dust thou art, and unto dust shalt thou return. (Genesis 3:14-19)

No man was able to escape the curse of God, because through Adam God made sure sin would be passed down from generation to generation. All men and women would be subject to the sin curse through birth.

Behold, I was shapen in iniquity, and in sin did my mother conceive me. (Psalms 51:5)

Wherefore, as by one man sin entered into the world, and death by sin; and so death passed upon all men, for that all have sinned: (For until the law sin was in the world: but sin is not imputed when there is no law. Nevertheless death reigned from Adam to Moses, even over them that had not sinned after the similitude of Adam's transgression, who is the figure of Him that was to come. But not as the offence, so also is the free gift. For if through the offence of one many be dead, much more the grace of God, and the gift by grace, which is by One Man, Jesus Christ, hath abounded unto many. And not as it was by one that sinned, so is the gift: for the judgment was by one to condemnation, but the free gift is of many offences unto justification. For if by one man's offence death reigned by One; much more they which receive

Chapter 7: The Effects Of Man's Sin In The Garden

> *abundance of grace and of the gift of righteousness shall reign in life by one, Jesus Christ.) Therefore as by the offence of one judgment came upon all men to condemnation; even so by the righteousness of One the free gift came upon all men unto justification of life. For as by one man's disobedience many were made sinners, so by the obedience of One shall many be made righteous. Moreover the law entered, that the offence might abound. But where sin abounded, grace did much more abound: That as sin hath reigned unto death, even so might grace reign through righteousness unto eternal life by Jesus Christ our Lord. (Romans 5:12-21)*

I have often wondered if this was the result of one man's sin, what is the effect each time we sin against God. Clearly we can see, by the previous passages, the price man paid for the rebellious act in the Garden has forever changed the fate of the entire human race. I believe we should be deeply concerned each time we sin against the Lord. In fact, sin should be a disturbing act that breaks our heart. We should be so caught up with living a victorious life that any sin, no matter who has committed it, should move us with sorrow.

Today, many Christians are immune to the act of sin. Open rebellion to the Word of God has no effect to speak of in the Christian community. Sadly, many churches take a spineless view of sin as well as its consequence. I wonder, for every sin committed today, how far does it set back our society? No man is an island to himself. Sin demands attention, even in our acclaimed but rightful Dispensation of Grace. We must never be so desensitized to believe we can escape the penalty for sin in our own life or those around us.

God is ready to help us triumph over the wiles of the devil. We must realize we are living in a wicked age, but through the Holy Spirit and His leading, we will have the faith to stand to the end. When we call out to God to help us in times we feel vulnerable to the devil, God is there to carry us through. There is more to faith than trying to receive that big answer. Faith should be applied in every situation we face throughout the day.

God is a twenty-four hour, seven day a week Lord, not one who is limited to a Sunday evening service, or some prayer-line. He is not some impartation in a revival. He does not tour with specific groups who feel entitled to His anointing or make claims to have exclusive rights to His awesome presence and power. He is omnipresent - He is everywhere my friend. He is here for you today and there for you tomorrow. No one denomination or group has exclusive rights to Him.

Beloved, we have the power to escape sin. Despite our contemporary approach to what has become a dirty word, holiness, God is holy. God is righteous. We must conform to His image. God is not interested in conforming Himself to fit into the relevant society in which we live. He is, He was, and He is to come. He does not change to fit into man's mold. God has given us His Word, a road map to escape the snares and pitfalls of sin. Through the Bible we have clear directions on how to overcome evil and bring positive change to this wicked and perverse generation. The Word gives power to transform the world into a better place, not to be conformed to the ways of the world.

> *Sanctify yourselves therefore, and be ye holy: for I am the LORD your God. (Leviticus 20:7)*
>
> *As obedient children, not fashioning yourselves according to the former lusts in your ignorance: But as He which hath called you is holy, so be ye holy in all manner of conversation; Because it is written, Be ye holy; for I am holy. (1 Peter 1:14-16)*

A college professor once told me holiness is God's standard of living. I have never forgotten that definition to this day. It is not a sign on the front of a church, it is not the dress code of a certain denomination, nor does it have to do with how much jewelry or makeup a person wears. It is God's standard of living. That standard should be the same standard we are seeking to live everyday at home, at work, and in church. Holiness is a beautiful word. It is a standard we all should be in pursuit of on this earth. And before any of us enter through the pearly gates, it will be our standard as well. You can be sure of that.

One may say, "I just can't live a holy life. I have tried and I just can't do it." I would first ask this question: Is the blood of Jesus sufficient enough to cleanse you from your sins? Is the power of His Blood sufficient to keep you from sinning? Is the Holy Spirit inside of you strong enough to prompt you to flee temptation? The answer is clear: yes, yes, and yes! The path to victory goes back to an age-old problem of standing firm and refusing to listen to the devil and his pack of lies.

Sin doesn't just happen. Salvation doesn't just happen. Crime doesn't just happen. Joy doesn't just happen. Everything has a process, and just for the record's sake, sin has its process as well. I never cease to be amazed at the excuses people give for their miserable stories of defeat with the devil. It seems everyone gets caught off guard these days and is forced into sin by Satan himself. Don't you love it when people stoop low and make lying accusations against the devil by stating, "Well the Devil made me do it!" Bologna! Let us look to the Word of God for a clear understanding of the pattern of sin.

> Let no man say when he is tempted, I am tempted of God: for God cannot be tempted with evil, neither tempteth He any man: But every man is tempted, when he is drawn away of his own lust, and enticed. Then when lust hath conceived, it bringeth forth sin: and sin, when it is finished, bringeth forth death. Do not err, my beloved brethren. (James 1:13-16)

As a minister I am very happy the above passage is found in the Bible. Even though the theology behind the passage is clear in many other passages, the fact the Bible comes right out and puts the point in plain English saves so much time. I know for many Pastors and Christian counselors it is so hard to get people to understand the Bible when it comes to confrontational passages dealing with their sins. People will use every excuse under the sun to dodge the Word of God.

Here is another passage that deals a hard blow to our comrades who like to lay in their sin and scream at the devil.

> There hath no temptation taken you but such as is common to man: but God is faithful, who will not suffer you to be tempted above that ye are able; but will with the temptation also make a way to escape, that ye may be able to bear it. Wherefore, my dearly beloved, flee from idolatry. (1 Corinthians 10:13-14)

Understand what the Bible is telling us about the fall of man; it has separated us from God. The fall made us a victim to sickness, suffering, and even death. It has brought curse and hard labor upon the entire human race. The fall eternally doomed mankind, removed all hope and made us servants of sin. We became stubborn and rebellious; our heart has become deceitful and evil in conscience. Women were cursed to suffer pain during childbirth (Gen. 3:15). The plant kingdom was changed forever by the fall. Man was forced to cultivate the earth by the sweat of his brow. He has to constantly cultivate the earth and separate useless weeds from grain and vegetables.

I would ask you this question: What has been the result of your sins? Where has sin taken you? How long have you suffered the consequences of one or more of your sins? Friend, we have God reaching out to us twenty-four hours a day. He is there waiting for us to take hold of His hand. He will give you the faith to withstand the enemy. The battle is won, faith has become a reality, the victory has already been won and declared. Apply faith and reach for deliverance now! One man's sin certainly affected your world, but your sins can be forgiven, and deliverance is yours from continual sin. Don't let your sin affect you, your loved ones, and your friends again. It's your Choice!

Today, reach out by Faith and come against all the Devil has stolen from you. Rebuke all the lies He has spoken to you. Sin has had a major effect over our Faith, but now it is time to understand that even though sin has had its physical and spiritual debilitating effect, as Christians we have been promised victory. By Faith lay claim to every inch of Promise land before you – Victory goes to the over comer.

Prayer:

Lord help me flee temptation. Give me the strength to withstand the enemy that would seek to destroy my soul. Give me the power to reach out to You in my temptation and say no to the sins of this world. Help me to stand firm on my faith. I realize the power of sin. I realize the consequence of man's sin. I claim the power of the blood of Jesus not only to cleanse me from my sin, but to set me free from sin as well. Amen.

8 | The Initial Will Of God For Man

So God created man in His own image, in the image of God created He him; male and female created He them. And God blessed them, and God said unto them, "Be fruitful, and multiply, and replenish the earth, and subdue it: and have dominion over the fish of the sea, and over the fowl of the air, and over every living thing that moveth upon the earth." (Genesis 1:27-28)

This passage is one of the most beautiful passages found in the whole Bible. Actually, it says it all in reference to what God's will was, and for the most part, still is for every man. I only wish man could really understand this passage today. I personally believe this passage to be one of the most feared passages by the Devil and one of the most forgotten passages by the church.

On one side of the coin, the devil does not want man to know he has a responsibility of fulfilling this passage (Genesis 1:27-28) today. On the other side of the coin, God wants His children to understand this command and know He is waiting to unleash all power if man will step up to the throne and accept this charge.

We should not feel alienated from God concerning this scripture; after all, we are created in the likeness of God. God does not want this passage to appear so ineffective in our generation. Does it sound strange to you the Lord is calling you and me to be fruitful, multiply, replenish, subdue, and have dominion? If it does, it shouldn't!

Chapter 8: The Initial Will Of God For Man

Beloved, there has never been a time in the history of man this passage has been under more threat by the Devil than now. The hard evidence is accumulating everyday around us if we will just open our eyes. While it does take spiritual eyes to see what I am talking about, a mere babe in Christ can and should be able to see the handwriting on the wall. What I am about to reveal to you may be shocking. When I finish with this chapter, I pray that even the most stiff-necked and mentally stubborn will see this passage in a way they may never have imagined.

Keep in mind God has just finished creation. God has blessed mankind and has given Adam and Eve specific orders. Now, remember this all important fact-- man is free of sin. Adam and Eve are living a wonderful life in the most beautiful place on the face of the earth - a paradise called the Garden of Eden. No devil to worry about, just man and woman living the way God had created them to live. There is no sin and the possibility of man sinning in the Garden does not exist in his mind.

At this point in creation God has supplied everything man needs to follow the command of Genesis 1:27-28. Man is blessed in the garden and He is essentially as free as a breeze, with the unlimited providence of God surrounding him day and night. Man is in perfect union with God and there is no obstruction between himself and God, hence, a Creator and His creation in perfect harmony.

At this point in time, man was living in his created purpose and there was absolutely no need for a Savior. That's right; you read correctly; man did not need a Savior at this time in his life. There was no need for him to be redeemed, reconciled, saved, etc., etc., etc., because he had committed NO sin. He didn't need the Holy Spirit to guide him because he communed with God personally. At this point in history, God was man's sole provider and protector.

Now, we need to draw several conclusions before moving on. First, God did not create man to fail Him. For some reason Christians today get the biggest kick out of thinking God intends for them to fail.

Secondly, God has never been amused by sin, nor will He ever! Our church today is sick with the most damnable doctrine - depicting man as this inadequate, pathetic, insecure spiritual bozo who has neither determination nor power to refuse to enter into sin. Such dogma can cause a church split, but the truth is the truth. We get all worked up in such doctrines as the security of the believer, or on the other hand, the insecurities of the believer; but God is not slack concerning sin, even among Christian people.

It is high time we understand the plan of God in our life. We need to concern ourselves with the will of God and leave those simpleton excuses we put up alone. Sin is inexcusable to God! Inexcusable! Inexcusable! It is an issue we face in our life. It is a fact every person must reckon with sooner or later, but the act of sin is inexcusable. In fact it doesn't matter who you are as far as God is concerned - saint or sinner! Sin is always inexcusable.

One fact needs to be made in reference to this chapter, and that is, even though God did not create man to fail Him, we must always understand one basic characteristic or attribute of God. He is Omniscient. God knows everything! People have argued for years over God knowing that man would let Him down and sin against him. The facts are, before the creation of man, God knew he would sin against Him in the Garden; therefore, a Savior would have to be offered for the human race. Of course we know that Savior as Jesus Christ, the Son of the Living God.

The assumption that a loving God would create man, put him in a beautiful garden, give him paradise, arrange an unavoidable decision to sin against Him, curse him, kick him out of the Garden, then say to him, I love you, and because I love you, I am going to make you to sin against Me so I can continue to chastise you the rest of your days, is absolutely ludicrous. Sadly, too many people believe this kind of sick humor and that God is the author of it. What kind of God would show such cruelty to His creation?

Let us see in the book of Romans how Paul explains the argument that God gets some kind of glory out of man sinning against Him.

> *God forbid: yea, let God be true, but every man a liar; as it is written, That thou mightest be justified in thy sayings, and mightest overcome when thou art judged. But if our unrighteousness commend the righteousness of God, what shall we say? Is God unrighteous who taketh vengeance? (I speak as a man) God forbid: for then how shall God judge the world? For if the truth of God hath more abounded through my lie unto His glory; why yet am I also judged as a sinner? And not rather, (as we be slanderously reported, and as some affirm that we say,) Let us do evil, that good may come? whose damnation is just. What then? are we better than they? No, in no wise: for we have before proved both Jews and Gentiles, that they are all under sin...(Romans 3:4-9)*

Chapter 8: The Initial Will Of God For Man

Why would some think God gets glory out of man failing Him? When I have the opportunity to dismantle such doctrine, I always take great pride in doing so. I love nothing more than sharing the real truth about a loving God and His Grace for such a reckless bunch of children. I always pray for God to give me boldness, and at the same time a heart of compassion, in dealing with the minds of saints which have been warped by such false doctrine.

I think many ministers and teachers of the Word have figured out, based on the Word of God, man had a problem living up to the standards of God in the Old and New Testament. Perhaps they have considered their own ups and downs in life (sins and problems), and figured there was no use in getting all carried away. God is forgiving and besides, it will all wash out in the end -- no use in expecting too much out of people. After all, if the minister can't live a descent lifestyle before the Lord why should anyone else be expected to? My friend, this rationale of spiritual teaching is one of many reasons our nation is in the shape it is.

Beloved, God is still the same in His approach to a sinful lifestyle. I know what some people are thinking right about now. You're right! The blood of Jesus has the power to cover your sin and he is faithful to forgive you of your sins, but friend, don't stop there. The Blood of Jesus also has the power to keep you from sinning.

Do you want to know what many people's problem is? They really don't have what it takes to stand against temptation. And if they continue in the way they are thinking, they never will. God is bigger than any problem. God is bigger than anyone's sins. God is not limited in His power to deliver one from temptation. God is in the delivering business. He can give you the strength to say no to the devil any day, any place, and any time. However, you must be willing to call on Him in your hour of temptation. Listen, for your own sakes, put a brake on it! Just say no to sin, and yes to the overcoming power of the blood of Jesus! Let your Faith be stirred in you and live in victory.

To really understand the point of this chapter, it is important a person consider the perfection of man before he sinned in the Garden. For a moment, put aside all knowledge of what things are like in this life. Put off all your cares, all your troubles, and all your worries. Now, focus on an age when man walked righteous before a Holy God.

The fact is, God gave Adam the charge of the human race and I am convinced by scripture the charge is still in effect today, except now the charge has been passed down to you and me. I believe the mind of God is still the same concerning His expectations of man. God has not changed His mind, nor will He ever do so. Scripture is adamant that God changes not-- He is the same today, yesterday and tomorrow.

Now, it is true because of man's sin the means of reaching God's expectations did change; after Adam's sin in the Garden the whole human race had to be reconciled to God. We needed to once again be brought into full communion with a holy, righteous, gracious and loving God. After a full communion, a process we call Salvation through a gift we call Grace, received by what we know as Faith, we were once again delivered to a state of innocence before God. Upon Salvation, we then were no longer guilty of sin nor the sin curse. We have been fully Justified before both God and man.

Yes, it is true, God was confronted with a real dilemma. Man, for the first time, decided to use a wonderful part of himself that God had perfectly created. In fact, it is the part of us that makes us unique to all other creation. It's a characteristic God even gave to the angels before He created man. God decided to put a free will in each one of us. God entrusted us with the responsibility of determining our actions. The Lord wanted a devout creation, not a robotic planetary human system in which the behavior pattern was dictated by Himself.

Even the angels of God had the ability to serve Him because they wanted to. They were free at any time to make a conscious decision to disobey Him (and some did). It is true, God, being Holy, demands a consequence for rebellion. At one time the Bible records one third of the angels siding with Lucifer in open rebellion against God:

> *And there appeared another wonder in heaven; and behold a great dragon, having seven heads and ten horns, and seven crowns upon his head. And his tail drew the third part of the stars of heaven... (Revelations 12:3-4)*

They were found guilty and were cast out of heaven forever. One must logically conclude the angels had the faculties to make decisions. Even in the Bible we read of angels making certain decisions, but they made the right decisions or they would have paid the price.

God is interested in honest sober decisions from a sovereign will in each individual. We do not serve Him because we have to; we serve Him because we choose to. We love God because we want to love Him, not because He

Chapter 8: The Initial Will Of God For Man

created something inside of us that forces us to. We were not genetically programmed to serve God-Jehovah.

Religion always comes easy to a race, creed, or culture of people. It's the name of Jesus that sets the world on fire and drives a sword between mother and daughter, father and son, and neighbor against neighbor. All God did was give us the ability to choose whether to love or hate; man has a free will and there is no scriptural (proof) evidence to prove otherwise.

Originally, man's only concern at the time of his creation was to fulfill that which he was commanded while he and God built a personal relationship. Once again, let us put everything into perspective here. God didn't have to prove Himself to man. Just how God and Adam cultivated a relationship is anyone's guess, but they had one, and because of man's free will it was mutual. I do know man has an innate instinct to congregate with similar and like-minded people and befriend them. It is only hate and prejudice that causes one person to hate another, and that is learned behavior, a behavior that was a result of the sin curse.

This sounds a little strange, but even today, man and God are alienated from one another. There is no inherited or genetic love between man and God, nor man and Christ. Only God has and demonstrates perfect love toward man. Man does not have love for God until he chooses to, but God loves man unconditionally even if He has to sentence him to an eternal burning Hell.

Only through Jesus Christ can man find God's love. Only through Salvation can a relationship be restored between man and God. As far as this great love affair ("love at first sight"), man and God will begin the relationship at the point of repentance. Let us look at these two passages.

We love Him, because He first loved us. (1 John 4:19)

But God commendeth His love toward us, in that, while we were yet sinners, Christ died for us. Much more then, being now justified by His blood, we shall be saved from wrath through Him. For if, when we were enemies, we were reconciled to God by the death of his Son, much more, being reconciled, we shall be saved by His life. (Romans 5:8-10)

Friend, isn't it great that God first loved us? Even when we hated Him and despised the church, even when as the passage says, "*we were enemies*", God loved us unconditionally. I realize this point may come as a shock to many, but the truth of this point, as you can see, bears witness with the Word of God. Certainly there is no other reference of truth than the Bible.

Now that we understand our position with God before the fall of man, let us continue on with the commands we were to fulfill before the fall. Here is a quick review of the commands: Be fruitful, multiply, replenish, subdue, and have dominion. We want to consider these words and their application to our own life as well as those of Adam and Eve.

The words "fruitful" and "multiply" definitely had to do with expansion of mankind on earth. It wasn't enough to multiply or replenish; God wanted a fruitful civilization of men and women. A tree can bear occasional fruit and produce offspring, but just because a tree may reproduce itself doesn't mean it is fruitful. The word "fruitful" in the Hebrew means to bear fruit, or bring forth fruit. I believe we need to return to God's initial commandment. Reproduction is vain in God's eyes if it isn't fruitful.

I am always amazed at the degeneration of our society as far as quality of life is concerned. Many people have no idea what a Christian upbringing is. For the most part, Judeo-Christian morals and ethics are no longer instilled in children. Boys and girls have been robbed of any knowledge of God in most state sponsored education systems. The blame, well, it's the parents fault. That's right; God never put the public school system in charge of raising your children and teaching them right and wrong.

The parents, not our school system is responsible for building character in our children. In fact it is up to both the mother and the father to instill moral character in a child. If there is an unfortunate single parent situation, the remaining parent has a double workload, and should receive assistance from family, friends and the Christian community.

The Bible is clear. Older Christians have a responsibility to teach younger Christians the ways of the faith. Sadly, God spoke this truth to His children in the Old Testament, but even they refused to follow the Word of the Lord. Man has always refused as a nation to do that which is right in the sight of the Lord for any length of time. We can see clear evidence of this point throughout the Old Testament.

Our own forefathers were steadfast in their faith in God. We see their rich faith manifested in the Constitution; yet today, men mock the very mention of God in any public gathering and public document. Let's consider what the Old and the New Testaments have to say about our subject.

> *And that ye may teach the children of Israel all the statutes which the LORD hath spoken unto them by the hand of Moses. (Leviticus 10:11)*

Chapter 8: The Initial Will Of God For Man

> *Specially the day that thou stoodest before the LORD thy God in Horeb, when the LORD said unto me, "Gather Me the people together, and I will make them hear My words, that they may learn to fear Me all the days that they shall live upon the earth, and that they may teach their children." And ye came near and stood under the mountain; and the mountain burned with fire unto the midst of heaven, with darkness, clouds, and thick darkness. (Deuteronomy 4:10-11)*

> *That they may teach the young women to be sober, to love their husbands, to love their children, To be discreet, chaste, keepers at home, good, obedient to their own husbands, that the Word of God be not blasphemed. Young men likewise exhort to be sober minded. In all things showing thyself a pattern of good works: in doctrine showing uncorruptness, gravity, sincerity, Sound speech, that cannot be condemned; that he that is of the contrary part may be ashamed, having no evil thing to say of you. (Titus 2:4-8)*

> *Train up a child in the way he should go: and when he is old, he will not depart from it. (Proverbs 22:6)*

Truly fruitful multiplying of the human race was God's plan instead of gross expansion of mankind without any hint of Godliness. My point is certainly confirmed in Genesis when God decided to destroy the whole human race except for Noah and his family. If God had been interested in population instead of the quality of population, He certainly would have taken another approach. In fact mankind was following His command in accordance with multiplying. The Word states men and women were giving in marriage; we all know what usually follows that event in a year or so.

> *And God saw that the wickedness of man was great in the earth, and that every imagination of the thoughts of his heart was only evil continually. And it repented the LORD that He had made man on the earth, and it grieved Him at His heart. And the LORD said, "I will destroy man whom I have created from the face of the earth; both man, and beast, and the creeping thing, and the fowls of the air; for it repenteth Me that I have made them." But Noah found grace in the eyes of the LORD. (Genesis 6:5-8)*

> *And as it was in the days of Noah, so shall it be also in the days of the Son of man. They did eat, they drank, they married wives, they were given in marriage, until the day that Noah entered into the ark, and the flood came, and destroyed them all. (Luke 17:26-27)*

According to scripture, it was important that man be fruitful and multiply; moreover, God gave us the ability and responsibility to populate this earth as well. The word "replenish" is interesting in its meaning, and often controversial in its theology. Without getting off the subject, I want to briefly introduce a definition of this word based on the Hebrew. Replenish means to fill or be full of. God wanted man to fill the earth with population, contrary to the modern teachings of environmentalists.

God wanted man to subdue the earth and bring it into subjection. In fact the word "subdue" means to tread down, to conquer, subjugate, etc. In short, we as humans were to be the masters of the earth - not the Devil nor the animals. Not only were we to be the masters of the earth, but according to the word dominion, we were to rule over the rest of creation. Creation is not to rule over mankind, but men being in submission to God are to rule over and master the earth, spreading the population all over, literally trying to fill the earth up.

Now, for the most important issue of the chapter, if God gave man this commandment in the beginning, does He expect us to carry on this command today? Yes. God gives us the ability to accomplish this command. Because it was a command to Adam and to the rest of the world, God will do everything He can to ensure man's protection while he obeys His command. Despite all the hoop-la, God is eager to see every man, woman, and child direct their energies to fulfilling the beautiful commission of mankind.

The secret to fulfilling this command is to live everyday in submission to the Lord, laboring in faith to fulfill His perfect will. God's commands are easy to fulfill if we will start within ourselves, obtaining God's perfect peace in our lives. We can have peace and contentment in our life if we are fulfilling His commands. We are to apply our faith daily in this fulfillment. There is no need to get worked up into a frenzy if we will walk in faith every day. It's all the little steps that matter in faith, not necessarily big ones. Steps upon a sure foundation are better than giant leaps of man on sinking sand.

I want to introduce you to a view of Gen 1:26-27, that you may not have ever noticed before. Remember the commands of the Lord, *"And God blessed them, and God said unto them, "Be fruitful, and multiply, and replenish the earth, and subdue it: and have dominion over the fish of the sea, and over the fowl of the air, and over every living thing that moveth upon the earth.""* I want you to understand one fact (if you haven't learned already): the Devil is opposed to every commandment of God. Friend, the

Chapter 8: The Initial Will Of God For Man

will of Satan is easy to figure out once you know what God's will is -- it's the opposite.

Beloved, anything against God's Word is always the will of Satan. When God's Word declares something is black, the devil reveals to his children it is white or gray and tries his best to beguile the children of God just the same. Often, when you feel the Lord speak to your heart and say, "Stop and wait on me," the devil will send tidings to move ahead – all is clear. He will do this through friends, family, and every other source, including masquerading as the prompting of the Holy Spirit in your life.

Sometimes the will of Satan seems to run parallel with God's, but anything off the track of God's Word is wrong, no matter how close it is. In the Old Testament there were times when God's children wanted to worship Him, but they decided to do it elsewhere than the place God directed. Imagine the worship of God being wrong. Yes it is, if it is out of line with what the Word declares. When God's Word declared come to Jerusalem and worship and let the high priest enter into the Holy of Holies once a year, that is what scripture meant. He didn't mean for some of His children to stop fifteen miles short and worship in Bethel.

Let us consider this passage in modern day terms. You may want to pinch yourself when I get finished with this chapter because you will realize how apparent the enemy has been in opposing this passage even in our own time. The Lord said first to man, "be fruitful". Not only is our generation not fruitful in the basic comprehension of the word, but it is out-right lazy. I can only wonder what could have made Sodom and Gomorrah worse when I consider the filth on our internet, television, in our schools, and on our streets. Where in the world have we gone wrong?

God's plans in the beginning were simple; yet through man's sins the possibilities of being truly fruitful have diminished drastically. The values of this generation are absolutely hideous in light of scripture. Man has gotten away from the absolutes of scripture and contaminated the truth with relevant thinking, "If it's good for me, then it has to be right." This path of living is in direct contrast to Christianity; therefore, it is against the Bible.

From the beginning of time, there has been a law that could not be swayed. There is a law that stands alone and above all others. There is a law that goes far beyond our Supreme Court, the United Nations, and any other earthly justice. There is a law which is natural and moral. A law that cannot be tainted by politics or money, because it WAS, IS, and shall BE! This law is God's law and it exceeds all laws of man.

The process of trying to get the law to conform to people's perverted ways is erroneous. God's law is straight and all must measure up to it. Absolutes are like plumb lines; just as a builder uses the plumb-line to determine what absolute vertical is, a child of God must use the plumb-line of scripture to determine what absolute truth is. Moreover, let's understand that truth is not partial or prejudiced, what is truth for one person is truth for the whole universe. There is no truth for you and truth for me; there is but one truth and that is the person of God and all He has declared. Friend, this is why we should live our lives constantly measuring ourselves up to the scripture, not trying to bend scripture to our inadequacies.

Today, most men and women no longer understand truth. Sadly, we see so many people publicly searching for truth in all the wrong places and people. Many of those who aren't searching believe right and wrong are a time and place in our past. Hollywood and other media outlets would have us to believe we have the ability to decide what is right and there is no absolute wrong.

We have allowed this world to try and tell us what is right. Most of our churches have stopped challenging absolutes because they also no longer know right from wrong. You can't know right if you are not willing to address and live above wrong. Compromise with the truth has produced a nation of people who are alienated from even learning the truth. What fruit do we see when we consider the values and morals of our children and our parents? God commanded we teach our children the ways of the Lord. Many years ago, educators who built much of this nation taught the Word of God throughout our schools and universities.

You see, the devil has confronted this commandment with subtle dismantling of values. For instance, children are given condoms instead of Bibles in our schools. Society pushes young couples into debt while they bow down to the god of materialism. We are consumed with sex and violence every day. Drugs and abuse are casually accepted like bad weather on the weekend. Our nation is in a welfare state, and there are more and more people receiving milk from our sacred cow, the government, than ever before.

Fruitful is a word challenged at every angle when considering the shape of the human race at present. It is not population that so much concerns God

Chapter 8: The Initial Will Of God For Man

in lieu of the fruitful; it is quality of population. We know for the past fifty years our nation, and even the rest of the world, has undergone spiritual bankruptcy. Without absolutes taught by the Word of God, our nation and our world is a sitting duck to the trickery and deceit of every foul spirit of hell. We must go back to the people we used to be before our legal system was hijacked by liberal minds seeking only to fulfill a wicked self-centered agenda that ultimately lifts up every hideous doctrine of the Devil.

The next command of God was for man to multiply. Not just multiply a desolate-minded race of people, but multiply a fruitful race of men, women, and children. The Israelites, at one time went to great extremes to teach their children the ways of the Lord. Great stories of how God led them out of Egypt were told for centuries. The stories of how God kept the Israelites' shoes from wearing out, and the way He fed them, were probably told around many tables and camp fires. However, due to Israel's continual sins from the influence of wicked nations all around, (nations which God had commanded them to destroy), the children began to go untaught concerning the ways of the Lord.

As idolatry was brought into the camps, (much of which was done by marrying outside of their own people), the parents, those who were Gentile and the backslidden Hebrews, had better things to do than teach their children the Law of God. People were soon consumed with their own selfish needs rather than the commands of God. As old as this story is, it sounds like our present day, does it not?

Today, thousands of years later, parents are still too busy to teach their children the Word of God. They are too busy to help their children with their homework as well; in fact, for many, they are just too busy for anything moral and decent anymore. There is, however, time to indulge in sins of the flesh and every godless act of immorality. There seems to be time for that adulterous relationship on the side, but not enough time to teach the children what is right and wrong.

Millenniums later, our economy is strategically fixed, to where both parents need to work to make ends meet, and children are caught in the middle of the great fight of custody. Will Satan win our children in the end, or will parents soon gain their children back when they realize they have been on one long ride that has led them ultimately nowhere?

I pray for the youth of America as well as for those across the world. Home wrecking is a real favorite pastime of the Devil. The more homes Satan can wreck, the more children he figures he may obtain as his servants. Statistics prove children brought up in broken and abusive homes are more likely to be physical, substance, and emotional abusers of themselves, as well as turning out to be common criminals.

You see, with our children being left alone at home for hours on end, Satan has taken the initiative to have them well taught by early adult years. He does this through Hollywood and our ever "dumbing" down of most schools. In fact, the other day, I read the quality time spent between a father and his son in teenage years is now less than a minute a day. All this plays upon the next command of God -- multiplying.

In a generation without knowledge of moral absolutes and full of selfishness, among many other sins, it is only conducive for them to get rid of anything that would interfere with their way of life. If it is an unwanted pregnancy, then abort it. What's the use in giving in to parenthood when there is so much to be discovered, so much to do in this world instead of spending time with a precious gift of God?

Our world thinks nothing of stabbing a pair of scissors through the base of the baby's skull and sucking the brain down a sink while the baby goes through spasms before its body is then removed another few inches out of the womb of the mother. Is this not the most barbaric act of humanity ever imagined since the time of man? And yet, we, as a nation, call ourselves civilized.

Then, there is what we now call "quality of life". Our elderly are now considered to be "in the way" of progress. Furthermore, they are of little use to anyone. Many think the elderly are merely using up precious natural resources that should be saved for generations to come. They are said to cost the consumers too much money in the area of medical insurance coverage. I have even heard it argued - because seniors are living longer and healthier lives - they are affecting the job market for younger skilled workers.

Slowly, we see trends all over the world that are moving to euthanasia. I read where in one European country the elderly fear for their own life when going to the hospital. There is evidence they are gotten rid of by lethal dosages of medication. This idea of trimming the population is even finding its hideous fangs in our government. No person has the right to judge the quality of life for another individual, but soon we will start to see more policy aimed in this direction.

Chapter 8: The Initial Will Of God For Man

To add insult to injury, we now have suicide doctors in the making. Going against all ethics of medicine, they would like nothing more than to help the ill choose to die through their machines of death, disguised as mercy. If America remains on this track, in the not so distant future you will see parents deciding the fate of their child based on ridiculous reasons, such as inconvenience, a disability, unexpected childhood illness, disease etc., etc., etc. Perhaps one day parents will conveniently drive their child to a clinic which specializes in permanently treating all "inconveniences" by putting them to sleep like maimed animals. The shame of it is, these clinics will most likely be funded by public tax dollars. My friend, where does it stop?

We find ourselves in this situation because men and women have neglected their moral and spiritual responsibilities. We have abandoned our Faith. It isn't God's fault we see this chapter alive all around us. It is our own. It is my fault and it is yours. If man had continued to obey God in the beginning, things would not have to be this way. If man would have stood firm in his faith, even after he sinned in the Garden, we would not find ourselves in this dilemma. We certainly cannot go back and change our past, but we can make a decision to no longer give in to the wiles of the devil and be defeated even further.

We can choose this day to set a new course for ourselves, and even our family. We can determine to start walking everyday in faith, letting each day build upon the day before, forming a sure and firm foundation. We must apply faith at this point and determine we will live up to the responsibilities set before us in the beginning. I will tell you this one thing: God is ready to take you by the hand if you will make that first step. Make a small step; don't worry about giant steps. Society has broken its own neck to get into the shape it's in, so with any movement in the opposite direction we are closer to becoming what God intended us to be than the day before.

Now, as we return to our topic, man is ready to replenish the earth according to scripture. God expected man not only to multiply, but he wanted man to fill the earth. God wanted men to separate from their own families and move out into the earth. God made the whole earth to be inhabited, but man often chose to hang around home rather than obey God.

I remember in scripture when God told Abraham to leave his own country He needed to get Abraham away from his family in order to equip him for the task ahead(See Gen. 12:1-5). Abraham left his country but took some of his folks with him. Then God determined He would have to get him off to himself, so it wasn't long before Abraham and his nephew Lot determined to split up for their own sakes. It was at that point God could speak to him concerning the Promise.

We even see another prime example in the Bible of this failure to migrate and replenish the earth(See Genesis 11:1-9). Remember when all the people decided to build a tower that would reach heaven? God decided to come down and destroy the tower of Babel and confuse the language of all the people so they would not be one giant body of a nation, but rather would move out and settle the whole earth. You know, God always has a way of taking care of things. In fact it is interesting to consider the ways God has worked around what seemed to be hopeless situations to bring about His will.

Think of all the times in your past God led you to the right spot or sent just the right person to help you when you needed it most. Maybe it was a situation you were unsure of, and all of a sudden God revealed the answer to you. Always remember, God will do everything to help you accomplish His will in your life. God has a purpose in your life and there isn't a devil in hell that can stop it from happening, if you are in sync with His will. The road may be rough, and most likely it will at certain times, but keep your faith, apply your faith, and take one solid step at a time.

As examined previously in this chapter, we have clear evidence how the devil has assaulted this command, as well as prior ones. I have noticed over the past decade global efforts to band migration into certain areas of the world; we hear much concerning the rain forests. Our recent administration has worked vigorously to stop progress in what is called protected areas and wet lands, and I have even heard of what is now designated as UN zones. You heard right. Right here in the United States our government is purchasing large blocks of land which will be used for everything else but populating.

What sense can the average person make of all these efforts? I often wonder myself when I consider all the news over the last several years. If it is not enough that we are looking at population control, there have also been extreme efforts to stop further expansion of our suburbs, and even, some charts to relocate people to certain designated zones! When God said to replenish the earth, that is what he meant, but apparently our society sees it differently. Once again, we see an orchestrated attack on God's Word.

Chapter 8: The Initial Will Of God For Man

God also wanted man to subdue the earth and have dominion over the rest of creation. In the Hebrew, the word subdue is: to conquer, bring into subjection. What an awesome responsibility for mankind to enforce upon earth. We are the conquerors of this earth. It is our responsibility to expand the communities and explore where no man has ever been.

Today, we see more and more environmentalists moving toward the idea that man is just one creation among millions of others. The word "creation" is inappropriate for their propaganda. To those whacked out liberals, man is just one notch, on the lengthy chain of evolution, right above or below the monkey. Many modern left-wing environmentalist "whackos" would have us to believe mankind is the most unstable and unprofitable of all life forms.

Some spiritually-minded environmentalists teach the whole universe is a god; each part of it contributes to one beautiful orchestra. Each species of life has its value and must be preserved even if it means destruction (infanticide, euthanasia etc.) of human life. How many times in our media have you seen thousands of people getting all worked up to save a beached whale? Meanwhile, only handfuls of people take the time to write politicians concerning the hideous murder of precious children through abortion.

Hundreds, if not thousands, of people will get all worked up over saving a fish said to be endangered. Liberals would rather see thousands of families out of work, to accommodate environmental extremists than to see some species of animal, such as the Spotted Owl, become extinct. Conservation is a wonderful act of responsibility and should be a goal for any family to take part in, but to equate man with varmints is anti-Christ, thus a direct assault on the Word of God.

Beloved, God's Word declares we are the masters of this earth, not creation. However, this is one area in which we have failed because of the subtlety of the Devil. Once again, Satan has sold us a poisoned bill of goods by deliberately going against the Word of God. Once again, the Lord put man, not creation, as the master over all the earth-- every corner.

Interestingly enough, there was a day the lion could lay down with the lamb. There was a day when animals shared the earth in peace and harmony. Man and beast ate of the herbs of the ground; it wasn't until man sinned that he became a carnivore. It wasn't until man sinned that the food chain was birthed. Beloved, here are the facts: man's sin has caused more destruction upon this earth than we will ever understand.

Today, God's command for us to have dominion over creation is an absolute joke to liberal extremists. The Devil has plotted with every rebellious pantheist to give sovereign rights to all of creation while limiting the rights of man. It is no secret the enemy seeks to utterly defy the Word of God. When we turn from the Creator to worship creation we are doomed as a nation. King David writes a beautiful psalm concerning this issue and puts it in great context.

> *O LORD our Lord, how excellent is thy name in all the earth! who hast set Thy glory above the heavens. Out of the mouth of babes and sucklings hast Thou ordained strength because of Thine enemies, that Thou mightest still the enemy and the avenger. When I consider Thy heavens, the work of Thy fingers, the moon and the stars, which Thou hast ordained; What is man, that Thou art mindful of him? and the son of man, that Thou visitest him? For Thou hast made him a little lower than the angels, and hast crowned him with glory and honour. Thou madest him to have dominion over the works of Thy hands; Thou hast put all things under his feet: All sheep and oxen, yea, and the beasts of the field; The fowl of the air, and the fish of the sea, and whatsoever passeth through the paths of the seas. O LORD our Lord, how excellent is Thy name in all the earth! (Psalms 8:1-9)*

My friend, when we see Genesis 1:27-28 in this light, it is interesting to try to figure out just what it will take for many of God's children to wake up and smell the coffee. Notice how craftily the Devil has made the desecration of the commandments a political issue. Some would say the church has no place in discussing such topics as abortion, environmental issues, population control, public education, or the United Nation's policy; however, these issues and many more affect the Christian community in every imaginable way. We, the Church, must once again address these sorts of issues if we are going to remain strong and have any decent legislation protected and/or passed. We cannot bow down to public pressure and anti-Christian policies any longer.

The Devil knows as long as the church sleeps, he can get away with anything. There are several reasons why these lies are going unchallenged. Many Christians live with their heads in the sand. Ministers fail to speak against controversial issues, while others have bought into the deceit. The news media and Hollywood have determined to set the course for society, instead of reflecting it.

Chapter 8: The Initial Will Of God For Man

However, here is good news, God is still in control and He still holds each family responsible for carrying out His commandments. Simple applied faith will see any Christian through in their attempt to overcome the status-quo and meet the responsibilities God has so wonderfully promised us strength to overcome. God's Word promises us victory against all enemies. Let us endeavor to facilitate total isolation of the lies of the Devil so we can show others the truth and point them to the straight and narrow.

Remember, if you are a Christian, God is committed to see you through in accomplishing His will. God is for us; He is not against us. It seems so many Christians go about their life as if God is just waiting to beat the daylights out of them if they fail. This rationale couldn't be further from the truth. God will do everything He can to see us happy, content, and full of peace and joy. He is our Heavenly Father, and He has the capacity to love us even greater than our earthly father could ever love us.

> *Moreover whom He did predestinate, them he also called: and whom He called, them He also justified: and whom He justified, them He also glorified. {31} What shall we then say to these things? If God be for us, who can be against us? {32} He that spared not His own Son, but delivered Him up for us all, how shall he not with Him also freely give us all things? (Romans 8:30-32)*

> *No weapon that is formed against thee shall prosper; and every tongue that shall rise against thee in judgment thou shalt condemn. This is the heritage of the servants of the LORD, and their righteousness is of Me, saith the LORD. (Isaiah 54:17)*

My friend, God has a plan for you and me. Though time has made its demands upon our lives, God's Word hasn't changed one bit. God's will for our lives, as pointed out in this chapter, is still as fresh, obtainable, and as delightful to entreat ourselves in as it was in the Garden of Eden. Once we have been redeemed from sin, God is there to take us by the hand and lead us to a fulfilling life on this earth. All we must do is lay aside the lies of the enemy and say: 'Lord, Help me to walk in Thy will from this day forward."

How do I apply this chapter to my life? First, realize God has a plan for your life. Secondly, know that God has given a command to all mankind – *"Be fruitful, and multiply, and replenish the earth, and subdue it: and have dominion over the fish of the sea, and over the fowl of the air, and over every living thing that moveth upon the earth."* Thirdly, know the devil has no power over your ability to complete God's will in your life, if you will pursue total obedience to God's will. With all this in mind, stand firmly on God's Word; this is the formula for applying your faith in this chapter.

Prayer:

Lord, give me the strength to accomplish that which was commanded of mankind in the Garden of Eden. Help me realize You have made a way for me to accomplish Your will in my life daily if I will live above temptation and sin. Let me realize I can live a victorious life on this earth through the power of the Holy Spirit residing in me. Amen.

9 | A Change Of Plans

Without a doubt, there isn't a Christian alive who would argue with God's decision to implement Grace over the Old Testament. I know I thank the Lord for His Grace in my life. If it were not for Him granting us unmerited favor we would certainly be in a real fix. The fact is if we were to get what we really deserve, we would all spend eternity in hell. I for one am thankful for the mercy of God -- aren't you?

It is important for us to understand we were created to live forever in a paradise made by God. Facts from previous chapters should have us in the right frame of mind to receive this chapter of the book. Because of man's sin, God was confronted with a situation He had not intended, but because He is all knowing (Omniscient), knew He would have to reckon with.

Prior to man's sin in the Garden, we stood before God without spot or blemish, but now we are all guilty of sin. Each one of us now have one thing in common, we are cursed with a sin we cannot shake off, outside of God's divine help. Our heart is now black, our soul is vexed with sin, and our flesh rebels against what is just, holy, and righteous. Man is in need of a divine work of restoration. Man is in need of redemption. What we now need is a Savior to redeem our soul from everlasting torment in a literal burning hell prepared for the devil and his angels (*Matthew 25:41*).

If man were to continue without a divine plan of redemption, he would live in misery on this earth, die, and take his plight through Hell's gates where he would eternally die in bitter torment. Imagine the whole population of earth living for nothing, only to die and burn in hell forever

Chapter 9: A Change Of Plans

and ever. Amazingly, each person is born to this ultimate fate; however, God has so wonderfully left man with a choice – Heaven or Hell or as one person once put it, Smoking or Non-Smoking!

Our fate was determined the moment we were conceived. Thousands of years ago, the love of a holy God sentenced every human being to death. That is right; the love of God is what passed a death sentence on every person. We would like to believe otherwise, but God is not hateful, He is loving. He is not unstable in His ways, but He is just, righteous and most of all, holy.

For those who are saved, they will avoid the cruel but deserved destiny awaiting mankind. Thankfully, God has made a way of escape for those who will simply make a decision to repent of their sins, apply Faith and confess Jesus Christ as their Savior. Though we deserve to be cast into Hell for eternity, God says there is another way. That way is through the blood of Jesus

I am so offended at preachers who continually preach a doctrine of the love of God without specifying the eternal consequences of sin. Today, we are plagued by a Pseudo-Gospel that will allow everyone to march in with the saints, but friends, that is contrary to the Word of God, and most of all, it is contrary to the nature of God. Man has a penalty to pay for his sin. The love of God both saves and condemns a person. It is the unfathomable love of our God that will judge and find every sinner guilty. It is an act of divine love to sentence every unsaved person to eternal Hell after they are properly judged and condemned to death.

> *And as it is appointed unto men once to die, but after this the judgment...(Hebrews 9:27)*

The Lord knew from the beginning He would have to offer man a way of restoration, while demanding death for the penalty of sin. Remember, God had just previously made mankind in His own image and blessed them. The word "bless" means to kneel as in adoration. Just how God blessed them is irrelevant to this issue, but they were blessed and divinely created in the image and likeness of God, unlike that of any other creation.

In all honesty, apart from the holiness of God, it would seem strange for God to create man, watch him multiply like the sands of the sea, and be cut off from His own blessed creation, whom He loved before we could ever love Him. The fact is, God cannot look upon sin, and neither can He allow it to multiply in heaven. What loneliness the Lord would feel not being able to walk with His most prized creation - man. What a tragedy it would have been for God, if it were not for Jesus Christ, the Savior of the World, redeeming man back to his sinless (meaning our righteousness through Christ) condition before a Holy Father.

I have always been a little amused, yet thankful, for the way great men of God have often argued with God concerning His plans to deal with the sins of the Israelites. I remember Moses pleading with God until the Bible says God repented, meaning He changed His mind. Of course, we know God didn't repent of sin; He merely changed course from what He originally had planned to do. Thank God for those who were willing to stick their necks out for what they thought was right.

According to the first part of Genesis, man was in serious trouble in the Garden of Eden. Both Adam and Eve made decisions to disobey God and eat of the forbidden fruit. It is true Eve was deceived and Adam sinned, but both produced a sin-cursed world because of their failure to hearken to the Word of God. It was by one man death was passed on to every human being.

> *Wherefore, as by one man sin entered into the world, and death by sin; and so death passed upon all men, for that all have sinned: (For until the law sin was in the world: but sin is not imputed when there is no law. Nevertheless death reigned from Adam to Moses, even over them that had not sinned after the similitude of Adam's transgression, who is the figure of Him that was to come. But not as the offence, so also is the free gift. For if through the offence of one many be dead, much more the grace of God, and the gift by grace, which is by One Man, Jesus Christ, hath abounded unto many. (Romans 5:12-15)*

What an incredible passage we read. One man's sin brought into the world a host of problems including sickness, death, sorrow, and pain. At the same time by one man, Jesus Christ, man can once again experience eternal life. By Grace man can live outside of God's condemnation. Man can once again have a fair chance to be found innocent of sin and set free from the curse through the redemption plan of Jesus Christ.

God loves His creation too much to see it all end before His eyes. What God has done through the years in response to one man's sins has been beautiful in anyone's eyes. God's plan to restore man back to his prior state before he sinned in the Garden is one of conquest. Redemption is a story of victory against Satan's desperate attempt to see God fail at His own

Chapter 9: A Change Of Plans

creation. The struggle to bring forth a plan of Grace took many thousands of years. Millions have given their lives for the cause, yet most have never understood the circumstances both man and God faced.

From the time man sinned in the Garden, God has been confronted with one failure after the other on man's part. It seemed with every move of God, there was always a counter move by the enemy. The fact is, our Lord, apart from being omniscient and omnipotent, has had to work through the free will of His own precious creation, man -- an amazing quest that is rarely understood by many Christians.

The process of redemption would have to start with one person, and then multiply into tens, hundreds, thousands and so forth. His plan would have to consist of a promise to man to ultimately bring about redemption. It would have to be a test of people's faith to receive the promise of God. Groundwork would have to be laid so man could not deny the legitimacy of a redemptive plan by our Lord. It would be a task that would take thousands of years, but in the end would bring about eternal salvation for any who would trust and obey.

The Lord would have to depend on one family to sustain a measure of purity to bring forth a Savior. While managing a strategic effort to bring forth a Redeemer, the Lord would have to establish a religious unit on earth that would epitomize the Person of God, in all characteristics. Because of the contaminated mind of man, God would have to reveal Himself in part by law. From the start He would choose to speak to His people through kings, priest, and prophets. In effect God would use seasons or dispensations to accomplish total reconciliation for mankind.

One other important note; it was not just man God wanted to redeem, but creation as well. Because of the sin of man, not only was man cursed, but also our entire universe was affected in some way or another. We often get caught up in the Salvation of a person's soul, but we also ultimately need a redeemed earth to sustain redeemed man. What we really need is for man to go back to his original created person before Adam and Eve sinned in the Garden. All forms of life must be redeemed as well to be able to accommodate a pure undefiled race of peoples.

The Lord has put forth a plan which will eventually restore the broken relationship of man and God. Through thousands of years of constant confrontations with the free will of man, God will carry out His final plans to secure man forever in a peaceful world to come. The plan of redemption is the will of our Lord. It is the heartbeat of the cosmos. Everything awaits that final moment when once again the Lord can look across the earth and all of its creation and say, "It is good!"

Friend, you and I are a part of this magnificent initiative of our Lord. Not only do we need Him for our Salvation and many, many other reasons, but He is looking to us for help. He is looking for individuals, families, churches, communities that will say to Him "I want to submit all of my talents, my qualities, and even my very existence to fulfill this master plan of redemption." It is up to you and me to say yes. Let's look to the Word for a few passages of scripture.

> *Trust in the LORD, and do good; so shalt thou dwell in the land, and verily thou shalt be fed. Delight thyself also in the LORD; and He shall give thee the desires of thine heart. Commit thy way unto the LORD; trust also in Him; and he shall bring it to pass. And He shall bring forth thy righteousness as the light, and thy judgment as the noonday. Rest in the LORD, and wait patiently for Him: fret not thyself because of him who prospereth in his way, because of the man who bringeth wicked devices to pass. Cease from anger, and forsake wrath: fret not thyself in any wise to do evil. For evildoers shall be cut off: but those that wait upon the LORD, they shall inherit the earth. (Psalms 37:3-9)*

> *In all thy ways acknowledge Him, and He shall direct thy paths. (Proverbs 3:6)*

It is important we realize this moment God is promising us something very special. All we have to do is apply our faith and receive our rewards. We know, based on this chapter, why we are in need of a Savior. He needs you and me to assist Him in doing so. How do we apply our faith? We are to search out what God would have us do to finish spreading the Gospel to the earth. When we act on this cause, He will supply our every need.

You see, as long as we are working on our own time, we have to pay the way. When we fumble on our own time, we have to suffer the consequences, but when we are working for the Master, we are on His time. In fact we are covered by the best "worker's comp" insurance in the business. If we take a fall on the job, He is there to pick us up and take care of us. We can even pay into a super pension plan. Every dollar we put into the kingdom is one God matches and multiplies back to us.

It is always God's perfect will for men to receive Christ into their lives so that they can be reconciled back to Him. After we receive Salvation, It is

Chapter 9: A Change Of Plans

God's will we venture out into the highways and byways to lead the lost to the saving knowledge of our Lord and Savior, Jesus Christ. We can be assured that if we step out and apply our faith to this end, God will lead us the rest of the way. We need not pray nor tarry on this matter; time is of the most importance. Millions are in need of Salvation. God needs a few good men (woman and children) to pick up the torch and lead others to Christ.

Prayer:

Lord, thanks so much for Your Love. I want to be part of the redemptive plan for mankind. I may not have much, but what I have I give to You this moment. I admit, I do have goals and even dreams. Teach me to put my wants and needs in spiritual order. I want to most of all be submissive to Your will for my life. I understand and accept in faith that if I will seek Your will first in my life, You will grant me the desires of my heart.

Lord, I want You first in my life from this point on; secondly, I want the lost to hear the gospel. I will settle for third place. Lord, help me live up to the responsibilities You have given me. Help me to become the person You want me to be. I want to live every day knowing I am fulfilling Your will in my life. Lord, I understand that I am a free moral agent and I have an innate will, but help me to be aware of the consequences of my will, so I seek out the bounty of living in Yours. I love You, Lord, and I need You to help me apply my faith every day that I may live up to my divinely given potential in Jesus' name. Amen.

10 | Why Hast Thou Forsaken Me?

Obstacles to our Faith

One of the biggest obstacles to the life of faith is managing to get over the thought, that at times, God has forsaken us. As silly as this may sound, it is a real issue in many people's lives. To be very candid, yours has most likely been no exception. I have talked with countless Christians who have wrestled with this dilemma many times. The answer is always the same; God has not forsaken you no matter what you think or how you feel.

There are a lot of promises made in the Bible. Many have tried to count them all. I have read several books and/or lists of the promises of God. However, I know one promise that I hold on to everyday. It doesn't matter how I feel, or what I have been through. I must KNOW that God has not abandoned me. He never has, nor shall He forsake me at any time.

> *Who shall separate us from the love of Christ? shall tribulation, or distress, or persecution, or famine, or nakedness, or peril, or sword? As it is written, For Thy sake we are killed all the day long; we are accounted as sheep for the slaughter. Nay, in all these things we are more than conquerors through Him that loved us. For I am persuaded, that neither death, nor life, nor angels, nor principalities, nor powers, nor things present, nor things to come, nor height, nor depth, nor any other creature, shall be able to separate us from the love of God, which is in Christ Jesus our Lord. (Rom 8:35-39)*

Chapter 10: Why Hast Thou Forsaken Me?

The fact is, my friend, it will be impossible to really grasp the whole idea of living a day to day life in the faith when you aren't sure if God is even there. The assurance that God will not abandon you is as important as the assurance God has saved you. What kind of God would we be serving if He were here one moment and gone fishing the next? That's not the Lord we serve - He is ever present with us through all trials and tribulations. He is God of the good times and God of the bad. He is God on the mountain, and God in the valley. He is God of the day, and God of the night.

Emotions certainly play a big factor when it comes to feeling the awesome sweet presence of God. Notice that word feeling. You can never put a lot of stock in feelings. Why? Feelings change from one minute to the next. For instance, I am a pretty happy-go-lucky fellow, however, as I write this chapter, I have been at home going on four days with the worse cold I have had in years. I feel bad. But life must go on despite my feelings or emotions. I would never want to make an important decision, nor should anyone else, while on OTC drugs, suffering with a cold.

There are many churches that are teaching an emotional experience with God. Frankly, I like to get excited about the presence of the Lord. Moreover, I love to feel His presence in a good service, or even during my own time in prayer or meditation. However, whether I feel Him or not has nothing to do with the fact He is still on the throne and even moving in my personal life. Even if it seems your prayers are bouncing off the ceiling and/or falling on deaf ears, it doesn't change one thing about the character of God - does it?

I had the opportunity to preach a message once entitled "My God, My God, why hast Thou forsaken me?" In this message I dealt with some of the realities and lessons we often believe about the presence and will of God in our lives. Let's consider this passage found in the Gospel of St. Matthew.

> *And about the ninth hour Jesus cried with a loud voice, saying, Eli, Eli, lama sabachthani? that is to say, My God, My God, why hast Thou forsaken Me?" (Matthew 27:46)*

These words mark some of the last words ever spoken by our Savior before He died on Calvary's Cross. In fact we will see that Jesus spoke to His Father, to man, and to creation as a whole. That day He asked one question before dying for you and me on the Cross. As we will look closely at the last comments made by our Lord and Savior, we will see a man continuing to reach out to others, even as many rejected Him that dark day on Golgotha's hill of sorrows.

Now Jesus makes two powerful statements to His Father while nailed to the cross. The first statement He makes is one of intercession for sinful man. Putting His own excruciating pain aside, Jesus remarks, *"Father forgive them they know not what they do."* My friend, Jesus is so loving that on the worst day of His life on earth, He had you and me on His mind. His obedience to His Father, and His determination to set us free from sin by His own life, superseded His own agonizing pain and torment.

Secondly, He makes a statement of obedience to His Father's will. Again, He says from the cross, *"Father, into Thy hands I commend My spirit."* Jesus knew in order to accomplish his Father's will, He would have to lay down His own life. He would have to make the greatest sacrifice one could ever make for another. Jesus laid aside all of His wants and dreams and followed His Father's plan. Jesus sacrificed His own life so that His Father could give us ours. What a story of love and heroism! Jesus had nothing to personally gain by laying down His life, other than the simple fact of fulfilling His Father's will.

As I recall this momentous time in our Savior's life, I am reminded we too must have the same spirit of obedience Jesus exemplified to the whole world as He died for you and me. We have to lay aside all of our wants and needs to follow God's will. We don't have to lay down our life and be crucified as a sacrifice; Christ has already paid the price for us.

As we look at our Savior's final moments on the cross, we can also see how He overcame the agony of crucifixion to speak to a perfect stranger and to His Mother. As most Christians should remember, thieves were hanging on both sides of Jesus. They were dying for their crimes against society. So not only is it important for us to understand Jesus walked and lived among the public, we must remember He died stretched out between two common convicted criminals who were guilty of their crime. Yet Jesus willingly gave His life, and was all the while innocent of any crime against man.

In a time many would have only focused on themselves, Jesus reached out to one of the thieves and pardoned him of his sin. Upon the thief's request of remembrance, Jesus remarked, *"Verily I say unto thee, today thou shalt be with Me in paradise."* What love our Savior demonstrated to the crowd around Him as they openly cursed and mocked Him before His Father as well as his own family below. My friend, Jesus reached out to others when most of us would have given up on everything.

Chapter 10: Why Hast Thou Forsaken Me?

By this act of love, Jesus gave us, as Christians, a model to follow during our time of persecution. He challenged us to look past our own suffering and continue to give to others right up till our own dying breath. We should always make time for others when it seems we are in our worst persecution and/or tribulation. In fact, often by focusing on someone else's problems we lose sight of our own miseries, and many times this action leads to the healing we are really seeking.

Not only did Jesus not give up on those around Him, but in the midst of His agonizing pain, He looked down and saw the virtuous woman His Father had chosen to bear Him. No doubt, Mary, the mother of Jesus, must have been heart-broken to see her Son stretched out to die in public humiliation. Only a mother could ever understand what a mother goes through in seeing her child die. I guess the saddest part of Mary beholding her Son's death was the feeling of utter helplessness. She stood below that rugged cross and could do nothing for her Child but watch Him die. She watched Him deliberately suffer for the sins of this world while He was totally sober and in His right mind. As her heart wrenched for the pain of her Child, the angry mob continued to jeer and mock her Son, as well as the Savior of the World.

One interesting point to note is the fact that Jesus could have taken an intoxicating poison to help relieve the pain of crucifixion. It was tradition to offer the victim of execution a drink made of vinegar mixed with gall. But after Jesus tasted the drink, He refused to accept the sedative, rather choosing to bear our sins in full pain. Why did He do this for you and me, my friend? It was to fulfill prophesy.

> *They gave Me also gall for My meat; and in My thirst they gave me vinegar to drink. (Psalms 69:21)*
>
> *They gave Him vinegar to drink mingled with gall: and when He had tasted thereof, He would not drink. (Matthew 27:34)*

At this point in His death, Jesus cried again with a loud voice and said, "*It is finished.*" For Jesus, His life was finished, but for us, our life had just begun. For approximately four thousand years man and God had been separated by sin's greatest consequence. For thousands of years God had planned for this very moment in time. All hell was watching as Jesus gave up the ghost in what was a torturous death on the Cross.

Little did they, the demons, realize before it was too late, that the sins of this world were about to be forgiven once and for all. The demons had no idea that the greatest act of God to redeem man was completed in the suffering death of His only begotten Son, a death Hell sought to arrange and deliver.

I will go as far as to say that if they would have known what was really happening on the Cross, they would have fought against God day and night to keep Jesus alive until this day. The Roman government would have never sentenced Him to death. The Devil would have sought to protect Jesus from the day He was born on this earth until now. Instead, they sought to kill Him from the time He was born until the day He openly and may I add willingly, laid down His life. The real fool in this story was the Devil himself.

Jesus, only moments from death, reaches out to His Father and asks the saddest question ever posed on earth, *"My God, My God why hast Thou forsaken Me?"* Beloved, God the Father openly turns His back on His Son. In a time that His mother was looking up to her Son in desperation praying that her Son's life could even yet be spared, His Father simply turns the other way. What a testimony of cruelty by His Father. That is right, during a time Jesus needed all the support He could get, His Father turns His back and forsakes His only begotten Son. What did Jesus do to deserve this hateful treatment by his Father?

Jesus was faithful his entire life to fulfilling His Father's will. Even as a child, at twelve years old, Jesus was consumed with His Father's business. No one knows of the times Jesus could have played in the streets with the other children, but like a good boy, He chose to study scripture and be about His calling.

There is no doubt at a young age Jesus knew He would have to lay down His life for all mankind. Having never displeased His Father, Jesus pursued His Father's will above His own wants and needs. I am sure Jesus probably thought about what it would be like to be a merchant, perhaps a carpenter like His dad Joseph. Jesus gave all earthly desires up to do one thing, and that was to live a life consecrated to fulfilling His Father's will.

Beloved, at a time in Jesus' life when He needed His Father's love and mercy, He was nowhere to be found. I am sure Jesus' heart must have been broken at this point. When looking down from the cross He saw those He had healed. He saw those who had been loosed from the Devil. He saw those who were once crippled and maimed with various illnesses. Perhaps He looked and saw those whose sight He had restored, joining in revelry and looking on this cruel scene.

Chapter 10: Why Hast Thou Forsaken Me?

Just days before this crucifixion, the would-be mobs welcomed Him into town as they shouted in the streets and laid palm branches down in His path. Now they cursed and mocked Him. As He looked down from the cross in excruciating pain He saw the world utterly betray Him.

> *On the next day much people that were come to the feast, when they heard that Jesus was coming to Jerusalem, Took branches of palm trees, and went forth to meet him, and cried, Hosanna: Blessed is the King of Israel that cometh in the name of the Lord. (John 12:12-13)*

> *Pilate saith unto them, What shall I do then with Jesus which is called Christ? They all say unto him, Let him be crucified. And the governor said, Why, what evil hath he done? But they cried out the more, saying, Let him be crucified. When Pilate saw that he could prevail nothing, but that rather a tumult was made, he took water, and washed his hands before the multitude, saying, I am innocent of the blood of this just person: see ye to it. Then answered all the people, and said, His blood be on us, and on our children. (Matthew 27:22-25)*

I can't imagine what it was like for Him to see this angry mob and yet be moved deep inside for the welfare of their soul. To add insult to injury, what kind of emotions do you think Jesus felt when He mustered enough energy from His beaten, scarred, bloody, shattered, suffocating, body, to look up and draw some relief from the presence of His Father, only to find He too had turned His back? The Father in heaven left His only begotten Son, Jesus Christ, alone to a vicious mob below. What heartache Jesus must have felt when He realized He was all alone! The One He loved most was nowhere to be found.

Let me ask you a question. Have you ever needed someone, only to find you were all alone? Have you ever needed your friends to be behind you, and then realize you were all by yourself? Has your family ever let you down? Have you ever felt the weight of what seemed like the whole world sitting on your shoulders? Have you ever gone out of your way to love and always do the right thing for everybody else, but when you needed one favor, you were all alone?

Have you ever felt like God had turned His back on you? Have you ever felt like you were out on a limb by yourself, only to look around and think God had led you out to die or be dismayed? Have you ever felt that the Heavens had turned to brass and God wasn't listening to a thing you were praying for?

I can assure you that many, if not all, Christians come to this point, usually early on in their walk with the Lord. The thought of abandonment is very common among Christians. We all come to those crossroads in our lives where everything is going wrong and God seems a million miles away. Beloved, just because something is common, doesn't make it a fact. Just because everyone has these emotions doesn't make it real. God is always there despite our feelings.

Consider these questions and statements. Why did the Father turn His back? Did Jesus sin? What did the Lord Jesus do to deserve the whole world turning against Him? Did Jesus ever let anyone down? Did He ever fail to put all others needs before His own? Did He ever act in a mean spirit that would have caused such a public outcry?

Beloved, Jesus had done nothing wrong, and yet He was forsaken by His Father and cursed by the crowd who maliciously stood below and openly mocked Him. He was totally innocent of any wrongdoing, yet He took the brunt of much hate on that dark day on Calvary's hill of sorrow. How could this happen to such an innocent person as the Son of Man? How could our Lord and Savior die in such a malicious way?

The reason is actually quite simple. Jesus had become sin, and as we know, the Father cannot look upon sin. Remember from previous chapters when we learned that sin always separates God from man? Well, the law still applied even to Jesus. As Jesus died for you and me He became Sin, understand me, He did not commit sin, He became sin.

> *For He hath made Him to be sin for us, who knew no sin; that we might be made the righteousness of God in Him. (2 Corinthians 5:21)*

> *Who His own self bare our sins in His own body on the tree, that we, being dead to sins, should live unto righteousness: by Whose stripes ye were healed. 25For ye were as sheep going astray; but are now returned unto the Shepherd and Bishop of your souls. (2 Peter 2:24-25)*

This chapter ends with three practical lessons you can build your faith on.

First Lesson

Feeling forsaken doesn't mean you are out of the will of God. Consider our Jesus as He was forsaken by even His own Father. Was He out of His Father's will? No. Absolutely not! The whole world is not going to herald you on in your walk with God. There will be times when your friends and even family will turn their back on you, or at least let you down. Don't expect a fanfare when you are doing God's will.

I would like to soften this point a little by adding that although your friends and family may not discourage you in your faith, they may not exactly lift you up when you need it. Often they won't share your enthusiasm about the things of God, hence, discouraging you a little and causing you to wonder about what you are doing and why the bother. I would like to encourage you to keep on keeping on for the faith. Don't worry about everyone else around you. You're the only one who has to answer to the Lord, not friends and family.

Second Lesson

At the Cross Jesus fulfilled the plan of God, yet in the end He was forsaken for a time. You will have times in your spiritual walk that you will feel all alone. The fact is you will never be alone, no matter how you feel. My friend, your feelings will let you down. Do NOT ever make decisions based on your emotions. Why? Emotions fluctuate for all kinds of reason. You may feel one way one moment and a change in temperature can have you angry and disgruntled in three minutes.

We must live by faith. Faith is not an emotion, or at least it shouldn't be. Yes, there will come days that you feel more faithful than others. There will be times you feel like you can demonstrate more faith than at other times. However, faith shouldn't be as the stock market - up one day and down another - faith should always be on the rise. What I am trying to say is - you just have to determine, and know that you know, that God is with you at all times no matter how you feel. Feelings will let you down when it comes to FAITH!

Third Lesson

You may feel like you are alone wandering without a cause, but if God has given you something to say or to do, don't wait on men to give you the floor. Go ahead and stand firm, even if it appears you are sinking – stay committed. Remember this, if God has called you, then He has equipped you, or He is equipping you. People will let you down. People will hold you up. People will often disagree. People change their minds. So don't worry about people, because you can't put all your trust in them to start with. Put your faith in God and be faithful to what He has called you to do, no matter how you feel or what others are telling you. Listen to what the scriptures have to say.

If we are in Christ we have an Advocate with the Father.

If we confess our sins, He is faithful and just to forgive us our sins, and to cleanse us from all unrighteousness. If we say that we have not sinned, we make Him a liar, and His word is not in us. (1 John 1:9-10)

My little children, these things write I unto you, that ye sin not. And if any man sin, we have an advocate with the Father, Jesus Christ the righteous: And He is the propitiation for our sins: and not for ours only, but also for the sins of the whole world. (1 John 2:1-2)

The fact is, if we are in Christ he will never leave us or forsake us.

There shall not any man be able to stand before thee all the days of thy life: as I was with Moses, so I will be with thee: I will not fail thee, nor forsake thee. (Joshua 1:5)

And David said to Solomon his son, Be strong and of good courage, and do it: fear not, nor be dismayed: for the LORD God, even my God, will be with thee; He will not fail thee, nor forsake thee, until thou hast finished all the work for the service of the house of the LORD. (1 Chronicles 28:20)

Let your conversation be without covetousness; and be content with such things as ye have: for He hath said, I will never leave thee, nor forsake thee. (Hebrews 13:5)

In the Old Testament you might say God worked in external ways. One's work was a testimony to others of their love for God. Today, we have the Holy Spirit living inside of us transforming us before the world, testifying we are Christians by the way we conform to the image of Christ. It wasn't until Jesus took on our sins and died for us on the Cross that the relationship could once again be opened between man and God. Unfortunately, for thousands of years God worked through kings, priest, and prophets. Now He works through each of His children, no matter what their vocation may be.

I believe that if God ever came to a crossroads in His eternal existence, it was this: Either I turn my back on My only begotten Son in Whom I am well pleased, or I turn My back forever on humanity which I created and love. Beloved, God's love is unselfish. By the Father turning His back only for hours as His Son bore our sins, He made a way that He would never have to turn His back on us again. In fact, if the whole human race would have accepted Christ as a propitiation for their sin, the Father would never have to turn His back on a single soul.

Chapter 10: Why Hast Thou Forsaken Me?

> *For when we were yet without strength, in due time Christ died for the ungodly. For scarcely for a righteous man will one die: yet peradventure for a good man some would even dare to die. But God commendeth His love toward us, in that, while we were yet sinners, Christ died for us. Much more then, being now justified by His blood, we shall be saved from wrath through Him. For if, when we were enemies, we were reconciled to God by the death of His Son, much more, being reconciled, we shall be saved by His life. And not only so, but we also joy in God through our Lord Jesus Christ, by Whom we have now received the atonement. (Romans 5:6-11)*

In conclusion, when Jesus was stretched out on the cross, everyone had forsaken Him, including many of His disciples, friends, those He had healed, and those who shouted when He came into town, as well as His Heavenly Father. Yet, Jesus Christ was completely in the perfect will of God the whole time. Just because things seem lonely and it appears the heavens have turned to brass, it doesn't mean what you are doing is out of the will of God. Sometimes heaven can seem very quiet.

Our Lord never challenged the will of His Father while on the cross. He was never hesitant concerning His mission on earth. Though friends, family, and most of all, His Father, had turned their backs, He maintained clear direction right up to the end. He willingly laid down His life as He fulfilled the greatest covenant that would ever be made.

My friend the crowd was right about one thing. He could have saved Himself. Instead He saved me, you, and all humanity. He could have called down ten thousand angels from heaven to loose Him and moreover, destroy that cruel hill called Golgotha. Jesus gave Himself to be tormented, beaten, bruised, scorned, and mocked so that in hours we would have victory over death, hell, and the grave.

> *Surely he hath borne our griefs, and carried our sorrows: yet we did esteem him stricken, smitten of God, and afflicted. But he was wounded for our transgressions, he was bruised for our iniquities: the chastisement of our peace was upon him; and with his stripes we are healed. (Isaiah 53:4-5)*

Serving God is much like this experience. Once you have determined that God has led you in a certain direction, stick to it, even when you might at times feel alienated from God. Do not go on emotions when it comes to serving God. If Christ had depended on emotions He would have turned back in the garden when all His friends failed to sit up with Him when He needed them most (Matthew 26:36-46).

Prayer:

Lord, help me to always know You are there, no matter what I am going through in my life. Give me strength to hold onto my faith when it seems everyone around me is pulling in a different direction. Grant me the ability to discern the right directions when I am at a crossroads in my life. Enable me by the power of Your Holy Spirit to stand tall and unmoved in my faith during trials and temptations. Lord, I know You are the source of my strength, which is why I call on You this day. Amen.

11 | Forsaken In Your Own Hometown

If God has you to do something and you are experiencing rejection, it doesn't make you any less effective than the prophets of old and our Lord, Jesus Christ. The religious as well as the heathen rejected them all. Your plight of faith and obedience will not differ from great men and women of God. There will be windows of time when there will be peace on the home front, and then there will be times when peace and contentment will be scarce.

> *And they were offended in Him. But Jesus said unto them, A prophet is not without honour, save in his own country, and in his own house. (Matthew 13: 57)*

Beloved, remember, the devil hates you. He wants to destroy you. He wants to see you fall. He wants to see you reject your Savior. He wants to see you deny the existence of God. He wants to see your faith shattered by overwhelming circumstances. He wants to see you be given over to fear and unbelief. He seeks to paralyze you with intimidation. He wants to see your family and loved ones despise you. My friend, the devil will do anything he can within his limits (determined by God), to crush your faith, and especially in front of others.

> *The thief cometh not, but for to steal, and to kill, and to destroy: I am come that they might have life, and that they might have it more abundantly. (John 10:10)*

> *Woe unto you, scribes and Pharisees, hypocrites! for ye are like unto whited sepulchres, which indeed appear beautiful outward, but are*

Chapter 11: Forsaken In Your Own Hometown

> *within full of dead men's bones, and of all uncleanness. Even so ye also outwardly appear righteous unto men, but within ye are full of hypocrisy and iniquity. Woe unto you, scribes and Pharisees, hypocrites! because ye build the tombs of the prophets, and garnish the sepulchres of the righteous, And say, If we had been in the days of our fathers, we would not have been partakers with them in the blood of the prophets. Wherefore ye be witnesses unto yourselves, that ye are the children of them which killed the prophets. Fill ye up then the measure of your fathers. Ye serpents, ye generation of vipers, how can ye escape the damnation of hell? Wherefore, behold, I send unto you prophets, and wise men, and scribes: and some of them ye shall kill and crucify; and some of them shall ye scourge in your synagogues, and persecute them from city to city: That upon you may come all the righteous blood shed upon the earth, from the blood of righteous Abel unto the blood of Zacharias son of Barachias, whom ye slew between the temple and the altar. Verily I say unto you, All these things shall come upon this generation. O Jerusalem, Jerusalem, thou that killest the prophets, and stonest them which are sent unto thee, how often would I have gathered thy children together, even as a hen gathereth her chickens under her wings, and ye would not! (Matthew 23: 27-37)*

There is a law when it comes to acceptance in your hometown. Simply put -- rejection! Don't think that you will be the first, nor will you be the last, to seek approval from your hometown. It is bad enough that we can often experience loneliness when it comes to our relationship with God, but if you are feeling rejected in your community, it is a normal and moreover, a direct fulfillment of prophesy.

Beloved, seeking acceptance is just pure human nature. No one in his right mind wants to be rejected. I hate being rejected -- it's humiliating. I wish everyone would believe me and trust in Christ as I witness to them. They don't. I wish loved ones would ally with me when God has spoken to me concerning a cause for the Gospel. Unfortunately, often our loved ones love us, but they will not always understand us, nor fall in love with what God has led us to do or say. Often what we have to do to fulfill God's will in our own lives differs from what others are doing and what they think we should be doing as well. When God moves on us to act upon His command, it may very well differ from how He has directed others.

> *Blessed are ye, when men shall hate you, and when they shall separate you from their company, and shall reproach you, and cast out your*

name as evil, for the Son of Man's sake. Rejoice ye in that day, and leap for joy: for, behold, your reward is great in heaven: for in the like manner did their fathers unto the prophets. Woe unto you, when all men shall speak well of you! for so did their fathers to the false prophets. But I say unto you which hear, Love your enemies, do good to them which hate you, Bless them that curse you, and pray for them which despitefully use you. And unto him that smiteth thee on the one cheek offer also the other; and him that taketh away thy cloak forbid not to take thy coat also. (Luke 6: 22,23,26-29)

The fact is, often the Lord will make demands on our life that keeps us on the cutting edge, and from being accepted by many. We shouldn't seek occasion to make enemies or be rude toward people, but the Word of God is powerful; it cuts deep into the emotions, leaving many defensive of their lifestyle. God didn't call us to make friends; He called us to be a witness. Some will never accept Jesus Christ as their Savior; therefore, they will reject not only the message of the Gospel, but the messenger as well.

Many could care less about the Gospel, our faith, and the fact we believe there is a God--they really don't care. Others make sport of Christians and their sincerity and sense of responsibility to the church. Then, there are those who seek occasion to bitterly attack Christians because of their faith. They attack verbally and even physically. They are not satisfied with simply mocking; they seek to do harm to those who would witness for the Lord. My friend, this group of men and women are dangerous and make completing God's will a real task.

Just remember, we are ambassadors for the Lord. We represent the Kingdom of God to this lost and dying world. Not only do we represent God, we can be sure He represents us as well. We cannot take the personal attacks against us by so-called friends, family, and foes to heart. We have been a given a measure of faith and we must use it for increasing and glorifying the Kingdom of God. Our faith must be strengthened by the Word foremost, not what others say. When we become dependent on the world around us for any assurance, it will lead us to eventually backslide, dry up, and literally lose heart in God and all that He is.

Friend, this world does not seek the truth. This world has itching ears for foolishness and fallacy. This world, including many of our own friends and family, seek after fables and myths (2 Timothy 4:3-4). They pursue useless tradition over a solemn or spectacular move of God in their midst. They would rather play childish games in the house of God than labor in prayer

Chapter 11: Forsaken In Your Own Hometown

for a heart-changing, soul saving revival. Prayer meetings are replaced with useless activities that bring no spiritual maturity to the believer. Bible study is replaced with protracted business meetings that should be conducted on other nights of the week or cancelled altogether.

As we move into a deep relationship of love and commitment to our Lord, we will surpass the spiritual walk of those we once thought we would never catch up with. It is not a game, nor is it a who's who in the church; it is a matter of fact, and when we find ourselves wholly committed to fulfilling God's will in our lives, it will rub others the wrong way. Some will be intimidated; others will feel threatened, while many will be filled with jealousy. Sadly, instead of rising to the occasion in pursuit of the same commitment, they will begin to harbor sinful thoughts of malice and hate.

The question is this: Should you allow yourself to cease from maturing in Christ in order to maintain relationships with people? No. Their friendship at the expense of your faith isn't worth friendship at all. It is your faith at stake, not theirs. You are to uphold the Word of God and continue in your faith no matter what others do around you, even if they are family members; remember where your true rewards lie.

Remember, my friend, if Jesus Christ and the prophets of old were not welcome in their own hometown, what makes you think you can do any better? If Jesus was persecuted for His faith, having never sinned against God or man, what will our own future hold? Yes, this is a hard look at truth, but remember the truth will set us free. Compromise is most often sin. One writer says it like this "Compromise is but the sacrifice of one right or good in the hope of retaining another—too often ending in the loss of both".

The Lord has called us to His purpose, not that of those around us. His desire is that we will forfeit our own rebellious will and submit to His. It is He that will never leave nor forsake us, not our friends and family. We are to focus ourselves on that which the Lord desires and be willing to forsake all others, and all obstacles standing in our way. Keeping the world happy about the work God is doing in and through us is not a priority in this age. Most could really care less about you and your God. We are to stay in tune with God and focused on fulfilling His will in our life. The Lord will grant us the faith to do His work.

God has called each of us out to spread the Gospel to this lost and dying world. Often it is very painful to have to look someone in the face and give them the unadulterated Word of God concerning their lifestyle and ultimate destiny. Even the sinner seeks approval in various forms; he is not immune to rejection. Often when the Word is applied, many take it as rejection and as a personal assault, rather than accepting the fact that you did not write the Word; you were merely spreading it to others in an attempt to be a willing servant in the eyes of our Lord and Savior.

Apply your faith regardless. Move with what you know is the will of God in your life, despite anything or anybody who would hinder you. If you are sure you are doing the will of God, then stand if you have to stand by yourself. If you can't get some respect from family and friends, then move on to those who will encourage you in the faith, after all, they are your true friends.

12 | God Wants Your Present, Not Your Past

As you should know by now, God has a plan for your life. His plan for your life is very special and can only be fulfilled by you alone. In fact you are distinctly different from your parents, your family and your friends. You are specially you. Whether your self-esteem is in balance or not, the fact is you are different from anyone else on this earth. That's right. Of the six billion plus persons walking on the face of this earth, God made you uniquely you; this alone should excite you.

I have had the opportunity to work quite a few odd jobs growing up, and I can remember never really being able to do any of my tasks as well as others around me. It seemed I always fell short of being the best or the quickest. I used to get so upset at others who always got finished with a chore, a race, or even a deadline before I did. It seemed no matter how hard I tried, I just could not compete with most people I knew.

Later, I found there were some things I could do better than the rest. You see, I didn't ever make the spelling bee, or pass with honors, but I soon realized I had a natural ability in art. Soon I realized I excelled with little effort in all my art projects. The fact is, if anyone beat me in my class, it was because I didn't give it all I had. Now, there were a few that hung with me, but even when I was in Drafting and Design, I remember my teacher giving me the highest grade on a project that he had ever given, up to that point in his teaching career. There was only one other person before me to receive an equivalent grade, and sadly he died in a tragic accident a few days before he graduated from school.

Chapter 12: God Wants Your Present, Not Your Past

The fact is God knows who you are. He knows all about your personality, your character, and of course all your secrets, including those sinful ones. He knows it all, but we can actually use this to our advantage. My friend, if God knows you that well, and He does, He also knows your strengths and weaknesses. He knows what you are capable of doing for the world and the Kingdom of God.

You see, when God makes a request of you, it may overwhelm you, but remember this one thing, if God has made a request, He has also given you, and will continue to give you, the ability and strength to carry out His request. Think of it, what kind of person would continue to make demands on people knowing they didn't have the ability to accomplish their given task? Imagine working for a boss who continually sought out ways to see you fail. What kind of person would he be in the eyes of his employees? Well, the same principle can be applied here, what kind of God are you and I serving – one who wants to see us succeed in ALL we do.

God has recruited each of us for a job, the Great Commission. Now, each of us plays a different role in this task. We will not necessarily have the same detail as the man, woman, or child around us, but we all are working on the same project. Seriously, has God called us to see us fail at this Great Commission? We have all been called by God, commissioned by Jesus Christ, and equipped by the Holy Spirit. There is no power in Hell that can stop us from forging on to victory except our own inabilities and failures. We stand in the way of utter defeat of the enemy. The enemy hasn't the power to stop what God has set in motion.

I was once told by a wonderful English teacher, whom I have come to greatly admire, that she had a desire to see all her students succeed no matter with what circumstances they were faced. She always said, "A person does what a person wants to do." The crude fact is that we are often our worst enemy. We stand in the way so often that it seems taboo to "Let go and let God." We would do well to give all our strengths, weaknesses, and fears over to the Lord. You and I are not strong enough to bear them alone. We must be vigilant about fulfilling the will of God and less concerned about our perceived inabilities.

One man said it like this, "whom God calls, He equips." I couldn't have said it any clearer. God doesn't make mistakes. He does not lie (Numbers 23:19). He is always perfect. He sees time from beginning to end. You and I are the ones so limited in sight. We see only the present and the past. All too many times we let the past dictate our future efforts. This couldn't be more dangerous for a Christian, letting the past control your future.

Beloved, look at your past, do you want to keep living the way you did yesterday? Do you want to go through the same trials you did years ago? Learn from your past and move on. You see, the past instills fear when it comes to applying your faith.

I once heard it said that a person has around 5000 thoughts a day. Can you imagine the poor researchers who worked on this project? Researchers found that about 75 - 80% of a person's thoughts were on the past. That is right, thinking back in their past - last week, last year, childhood, or even five minutes ago.

You can't change one thing in your past, not one thing. Learn from it, and let the past die. Bury all those old memories that are not pure and holy. You don't need the extra luggage for the journey ahead that God has called you to. It is too much to tote on this pilgrimage in this span we call life. Free yourself so you can run the race which is set before you. You can't afford to stall in your efforts to serve God and reminisce about things that have no value, but rather slow you down so you can get depressed and have pity parties.

It is true that often God can use a person who has come through certain situations in their lives, either after they got saved or before, to help others come through them too. We grow in the Lord, and along life's way we have plenty of opportunities to mess things up. We can often use our mistakes and failures to help head others off from making the same errors we did. Sadly, many will not listen to you and will go down the same road, ignoring your heart-felt advice to them.

Simply put, use your past to benefit others in their everyday faith. Don't let your past bring dismay to you who are living a faithful life to our Lord and Savior. Remember, He has put all your past behind you and covered it by the shed blood of Jesus Christ. So, what business is it of ours to be digging when God has buried our past?

Dead things are of no value to the living when it comes to your faith. If it is dead and you cannot resurrect it, leave it. Flee for your own good, or you may become contaminated with the rot of this world. The past is the past, it is under the Blood now, and God has called you out from this world. Arm yourself with the spiritual warfare needed to fight against the devil.

Chapter 12: God Wants Your Present, Not Your Past

Finally, my brethren, be strong in the Lord, and in the power of His might. Put on the whole armour of God, that ye may be able to stand against the wiles of the devil. For we wrestle not against flesh and blood, but against principalities, against powers, against the rulers of the darkness of this world, against spiritual wickedness in high places. Wherefore take unto you the whole armour of God, that ye may be able to withstand in the evil day, and having done all, to stand. Stand therefore, having your loins girt about with truth, and having on the breastplate of righteousness; And your feet shod with the preparation of the gospel of peace; Above all, taking the shield of faith, wherewith ye shall be able to quench all the fiery darts of the wicked. And take the helmet of salvation, and the sword of the Spirit, which is the Word of God: Praying always with all prayer and supplication in the Spirit, and watching thereunto with all perseverance and supplication for all saints; (Ephesians 6: 10-18)

Yes, God made you uniquely different; your ideas about what others think of you are worthless moments of time in which you could have been doing something constructive for the Kingdom of God. I leave you with this thought: if God has created you special, and if He has called you to exercise your faith for the fulfillment of His will in your life, who are you to even ponder the idea of second guessing the Lord God Almighty? Beloved, God is our best friend. He desires to see us prosper and succeed in all that we do. He is for us, not against us.

What shall we then say to these things? If God be for us, who can be against us? (Romans 8:31)

Prayer:

Dear Lord, help me to overcome areas of fear and doubt in my life. Help me to realize You have given me the resources to do Your work. Let me be confident in the person You created me to be. Deliver me from any attack of depression Satan would try to bring into my life by reminding me of my past failures. I will lean on You, Lord, to be my Strength and Shield in the work ahead. In Jesus name, Amen.

13 | DNA And Faith

One of the greatest attributes of God is the fact He is omniscient. This means He knows everything. Yes, I mean God knows everything there is to know. He is the great architect of this universe, as well as the great engineer of the human body. There are no accidents when it comes to the Lord's work. I believe every created thing has a purpose and place in society. Furthermore, I sincerely believe with all of my heart God is a God of economy; He wastes nothing.

> *To every thing there is a season, and a time to every purpose under the heaven: A time to be born, and a time to die; a time to plant, and a time to pluck up that which is planted; A time to kill, and a time to heal; a time to break down, and a time to build up; A time to weep, and a time to laugh; a time to mourn, and a time to dance; A time to cast away stones, and a time to gather stones together; a time to embrace, and a time to refrain from embracing; A time to get, and a time to lose; a time to keep, and a time to cast away; A time to rend, and a time to sew; a time to keep silence, and a time to speak; A time to love, and a time to hate; a time of war, and a time of peace. (Ecclesiastes 3:1-8)*

When something has lost its purpose with God, it is either destroyed for good reason or made into something that will fulfill another purpose. God knows you and knows your days and nights. He even knows the hairs on your head, as well as the sparrows that fall from the sky. You will never fall off the face of the earth without God's prior knowledge. He will keep you safe and secure all the days of your life. He loves you and is concerned about the smallest details of your overall welfare.

Chapter 13: DNA And Faith

> *Are not two sparrows sold for a farthing? and one of them shall not fall on the ground without your Father. But the very hairs of your head are all numbered. Fear ye not therefore, ye are of more value than many sparrows. (Matthew 10:29-31)*

Our purpose on earth is very clear when it comes to the Lord and His will for our life. It is, however, worth mentioning that we, as humans, often slow, hinder, or completely annihilate the perfect will of God in our lives with our blunders, failures, impatience and sin. This action isn't the work of God, but the work of our own actions over those of God. In short, God's own servants (Christians) often hinder His will.

This fact is exposed in the Lord's Prayer. Consider the words, *"Thy kingdom come. Thy will be done in earth, as it is in heaven (Matthew 6: 10)."* If the will of God was decided and without need of prayer, than why would we be requested to pray for it *"in earth"* as it is in heaven? Certainly the Lord would not contradict Himself when He reminds us of the prayers of the heathen.

> *But when ye pray, use not vain repetitions, as the heathen do: for they think that they shall be heard for their much speaking. (Matthew 6:7)*

Notice in heaven the will of God is of little issue as far as its fulfillment, but beloved, even the Lord is requesting our attention be given to completing His will on earth. Now, this is no accident or waste of words. This prayer was a model set forth by Jesus to His disciples and the world afterward. We are to model our prayers after this beautiful prayer He offered up and set forth as an example for His disciples.

Now, we come to a very complex study of how far and deep God will go in nurturing the right person for a specific task in the fulfillment of His will. We will see clearly how we can stand and simply exercise our faith in the knowledge that God didn't start yesterday working in us the necessary qualities to carry out His plan, but rather started at our conception, designing us to be His servant and vessel for the fulfillment of His divine will and purpose.

First, God wonderfully made you before you were even born. That is right. He crafted you and knew you before you ever saw the light of day. You are made in His image and crafted together for His divine purpose. Let's consider the Scripture below and examine the point I am asserting.

> *O LORD, Thou hast searched me, and known me. Verse 14, I will praise Thee; for I am fearfully and wonderfully made: marvellous are Thy works;*

and that my soul knoweth right well. My substance was not hid from Thee, when I was made in secret, and curiously wrought in the lowest parts of the earth. Thine eyes did see my substance, yet being unperfect; and in Thy book all my members were written, which in continuance were fashioned, when as yet there was none of them. (Psalms 139 portion)

As we learn to understand the very attributes of God while we seek to build our faith, it is fundamentally important we understand His omniscience (He knows all things). This point was made earlier. When I say "knows everything" I mean He knows everything about everything. "All things" means all things; the Lord knows the past, the present and the future. He sees the future as well as the present.

It is evident according to Scripture, God will search out things, but that doesn't exclude Him from knowing all things. Some have said He limits His knowledge. Well that is His option, but it doesn't change the fact all knowledge is His to know. Let us consider how God searched out David according to Psalms 139.

O LORD, Thou hast searched me, and known me. Thou knowest my downsitting and mine uprising, Thou understandest my thought afar off. Thou compassest my path and my lying down, and art acquainted with all my ways. For there is not a word in my tongue, but, lo, O LORD, Thou knowest it altogether. Thou hast beset me behind and before, and laid Thine hand upon me. Such knowledge is too wonderful for me; it is high, I cannot attain unto it. Whither shall I go from Thy spirit? or whither shall I flee from thy presence? If I ascend up into heaven, Thou art there: if I make my bed in hell, behold, Thou art there. If I take the wings of the morning, and dwell in the uttermost parts of the sea; Even there shall Thy hand lead me, and Thy right hand shall hold me. If I say, Surely the darkness shall cover me; even the night shall be light about me. Yea, the darkness hideth not from Thee; but the night shineth as the day: the darkness and the light are both alike to Thee. For Thou hast possessed my reins: Thou hast covered me in my mother's womb. I will praise Thee; for I am fearfully and wonderfully made: marvellous are Thy works; and that my soul knoweth right well. My substance was not hid from Thee, when I was made in secret, and curiously wrought in the lowest parts of the earth. Thine eyes did see my substance, yet being unperfect; and in Thy book all my members were written, which in continuance were fashioned, when as yet there was none of them. How precious also are Thy thoughts unto me, O God! how great is the sum of

Chapter 13: DNA And Faith

them! If I should count them, they are more in number than the sand: when I awake, I am still with Thee. Surely Thou wilt slay the wicked, O God: depart from me therefore, ye bloody men. For they speak against Thee wickedly, and Thine enemies take Thy name in vain. Do not I hate them, O LORD, that hate Thee? and am not I grieved with those that rise up against Thee? I hate them with perfect hatred: I count them mine enemies. Search me, O God, and know my heart: try me, and know my thoughts: And see if there be any wicked way in me, and lead me in the way everlasting.

In this wonderful chapter of Psalms 139, we see sixteen ways that God sought knowing His servant David. Below is a list of these ways:

- Searched me
- Known me.
- Known my downsitting.
- Known my uprising.
- Understood my thoughts afar off.
- Compassed my path.
- Compassed my lying down.
- Became acquainted with all my ways.
- Known every word in my tongue.
- Beset me from behind.
- Beset me before.
- Laid His hand upon me.
- Possessed my reins.
- Covered me in my mother's womb.
- Seen my substance when I was forming in my mother's womb.
- Written all my members in a book.

Notice that God's knowledge of man is declared in his formation, all his thoughts, his purpose, and the providence of God over his life, but nothing is said concerning God's omniscience regarding the preexistence of a man.

So what about DNA (*deoxyribonucleic acid*)? What does DNA have to do with God? My friend you might be surprised to find God was in the DNA business long before science got there. God was in the genetics business before science ever mapped our "Code." God knows all things and is the mastermind behind all creation. Researchers will never, I say never, pull one off on our Lord. So many positive discoveries have only been a testimony to the authority and divine inspiration of God's Word.

Friend, the color of your skin, the color of your eyes, the number of hairs you have, is all privy to God. He designed you. You're not a freak. It doesn't matter what you think about how you look or the disabilities you may have, God knew you before you were ever born. As complex as the human body is, God has you figured out right down to the length of your toes.

I believe one may be thinking at this moment if God knows everything, then why didn't He stop the mother from giving birth to the severely handicapped. A child who would only live for six months and cause all kinds of hardship on the parents, as well as financial strain on the marriage? Friend, dare to ask our Lord, but be prepared for the answers He may give. God is not too big, nor too small to answer your questions, no matter what the case may be.

To answer the question you posed, I don't know the answer. There may be several reasons why God would allow such a thing. We may consider these observations of truth: We live in a cursed world. We live and breathe in a body that has a sin curse upon it; one that is mortal and corruptible. We face the law of the harvest - we reap what we sow!

One pastor said it like this: "There is a grace we have to die by and a grace we have to live by." God is there for us in all our times of need. We may never have all the whys answered in our lifetime, but I know this fact, as long as you and I live and breathe the air, we will be susceptible to many things around us.

There will come that day in the future when we will be changed in the twinkling of an eye. This old body will be changed from corruptible to incorruptible, from mortal to immortal. That day will come to pass, and when it does, we will care less about those unanswered questions. Beloved, I can't wait till that day.

> *Behold, I show you a mystery; We shall not all sleep, but we shall all be changed, In a moment, in the twinkling of an eye, at the last trump: for the trumpet shall sound, and the dead shall be raised incorruptible, and we shall be changed. For this corruptible must put on incorruption, and this mortal must put on immortality. So when this corruptible shall have put on incorruption, and this mortal shall have put on immortality, then shall be brought to pass the saying that is written, Death is swallowed*

Chapter 13: DNA And Faith

> up in victory. O death, where is thy sting? O grave, where is thy victory? (1 Corinthians 15: 51-55)

First, let us define DNA (deoxyribonucleic acid), "It is a nucleic acid that carries the genetic information which determines individual hereditary characteristics, consists of two long chains of nucleotides twisted into a double helix, and is the major constituent of chromosomes." (Microsoft Encarta 98 Encyclopedia)

Don't ask me to explain DNA scientifically, but what I will attempt to do is to show you God was using it long before scientists were. I will attempt to prove God not only had the *Genetic Code* written down, but also used it in our creation. I will thus prove God is much more advanced than any issue of Science Digest.

> *My substance was not hid from Thee, when I was made in secret, and curiously wrought in the lowest parts of the earth. Thine eyes did see my substance, yet being unperfect; and in Thy book all my members were written, which in continuance were fashioned, when as yet there was none of them. (Psalms 139:15-16)*

As we progress in this exciting discovery of God's omniscience, we must continue to define certain words that give this thesis the structure and credibility it needs to bring about a burst of faith to any Christian and an iron clad defense against all skeptics. Below are seven words found in this passage that expose facts that I seek to assert.

Substance: Bone structure, external covering of muscular flesh, tendons, veins, arteries, nerves, and skin.

Wrought: to variegate color, i.e. embroider; by impl. to fabricate:-- embroidered needlework.

Substance (2nd use of the word): golem, a wrapped (and unformed mass, i.e. as the embryo):--substance yet being unperfect.

Unperfect: not formed yet, without structure.

Members: Parts of the body.

Continuance: Day by day.

Fashioned: Squeezed and molded as like unto a potter.

Now, we will go through this passage again, only I have inserted the definitions into the text to make the point. (Ps 139:15-16) *My <u>substance</u>*

"flesh and bone" *was not hid from thee, when I was made in* <u>secret</u> "unknown to any", *and* <u>curiously wrought</u> "my body was developed one cell at a time" *in the* <u>lowest parts</u> "in my mothers womb" *of the earth. Thine eyes did see my* <u>substance</u> "embryo", *yet being* <u>unperfect</u> "nothing"; *and in thy* <u>book</u> "genetic code register" <u>all</u> "complete" *my* <u>members</u> "parts of the body" *were written, which in* <u>continuance</u> "day by day" *were* <u>fashioned</u> "squeezed and molded", *when as yet there was* <u>none of them</u> "before I was born".

Please allow me to translate all this together and put it into sentence form again. "My flesh and bone was not hid from You. When I was unknown to any and developed one cell at a time in my mother's womb, You saw me as an embryo being nothing, and You registered every part of my body and saw me grow day by day being squeezed and molded together before I was ever born".

My friend, in heaven there is a book or a record that has written the whole account of your birth, from conception to cemetery. Your body was recorded day by day, your bright eyes, your long nose, your freckles, your big feet, and your short fingers. It's all there, and God wrote it. Beloved, no matter what state of mind you are in, no matter what deformity affects you every day, God either authored it, or due to circumstance, allowed it.

The next time someone makes fun of you because of what they perceive as a defect, be reminded that God, in His infinite wisdom, noted that part of your body that others seem to laugh at. I would add this; they are actually making fun of God's work, His craftsmanship. This is a good reason we should never make fun of others, nor ever tolerate our children calling people names, especially when the names are making fun of a person's appearance or level of mental development as we perceive it.

Name-calling is very cruel. It cuts deep and leaves scars that often last for many years, even years into adulthood. People cannot help the way they look. They cannot often help their level of intelligence or IQ. The fact is, we are not responsible for God's work. Inside each person is a treasure to be unleashed and discovered. We all have within us the ability to build a better home, community, and world in which we live. God made you like that, so stop complaining about yourself, and certainly never make fun of others.

So, in conclusion we can't change who we are, but we can change where we are going! Scientist tells us one day they will be able to determine various strings of cancers and other diseases by observing our genetic code.

Chapter 13: DNA And Faith

All I have to say to that is, we all have an appointment with death, and we will NOT be one moment early nor late.

And as it is appointed unto men once to die, but after this the judgment: (Hebrews 9:27)

How about this question: Are you ready for your appointment? Is your family ready for theirs?

Application of faith is made easy when we realize that God truly does understand all things and is aware of all things in our life, right down to our creation. The physical or mental inadequacies you feel you have are, first of all, part of who you may be. Second of all, are you sure you have "inadequacies" or, are you trying to see yourself through what others perceive?

Don't let Hollywood or some foolish magazine written by a bunch of scripturally ignorant people dictate what you should look like and what you should wear. What they accept as fashionable and intelligent, God's Word often deems as foolish. Be the perfect individual God crafted you to be. Break loose and discover the paths God wants you to follow. God doesn't need another empty sociological mime.

Prayer:

Lord, help us to be content in all that we have, in all that we are, despite the misfortunes, and the inabilities we may feel we have. Let us be mindful of those around us that are less fortunate as we see them, but uniquely made as You know them. Allow faith to build inside of us, that we can know that we are wonderfully made, and that You, Lord, know the very number of cells in our body, as well as what tomorrow brings. Amen..

14 | God Never Changes, People Do

One of the fundamental foundations of our faith is the fact God never changes. Every minute brings on new challenges to our faith in God, but we must remain steadfast in the knowledge that despite the circumstances around us, God doesn't change.

Change is a word we have grown accustomed to. Desirable by many, and detested by others, change is a fact of life. There are varieties we must all learn to face. For each person the certainty of death lurks with each tick of the clock. As the clock makes its round we all, unfortunately, draw closer to death.

On our often precarious pilgrimage through life, from cradle to grave, situations will affront us, even overwhelm us at times. Despite the overwhelming situations we all must endure, our faith demands we draw strength from One who knows no change. We are reminded in Malachi, 3:6a, *"For I am the LORD, I change not..."* As Christians we can draw strength and assurance in this verse. As humans, change is inevitable, with God, He changes not.

On the dresser in our master bedroom is displayed two beautifully framed pictures of Darlene and I when we were babies. Our appearance has changed tremendously. We are much older and I am not as cute anymore. My wife, however, is. Time, hard work, stress, and most of all age has taken its toll on our appearance. This "Oil of Olay" society isn't as happy about growing older as some used to be. We simply pass this change off as maturity, but change it is.

On the other hand, God is still the same. We have no pictures or recollections of Jesus as a child. There are no stories of Him going through

Chapter 14: God Never Changes, People Do

the "terrible twos." Scripture doesn't record His struggle with teething and prolonged hours of crying with the tummy ache, that is, if He had one at all. We simply accept Him as God. We are instructed He is the Great I Am, the Alpha and Omega, the Beginning and the End, simply put, we never question.

To understand our passage from Malachi 3:6, we need to look at this verse in context. In the preceding verse we see particular sins and behaviors ferreted out before the children of God by Malachi the prophet.

And I will come near to you to judgment; and I will be a swift witness against the sorcerers, and against the adulterers, and against false swearers, and against those that oppress the hireling in his wages, the widow, and the fatherless, and that turn aside the stranger from his right, and fear not Me, saith the LORD of hosts. (Malachi 3:5)

As outlined by Scripture, God was about to judge the sorcerers, adulterers, false swearers, and oppressors. The Scripture is adamant concerning the sins of Israel in this passage. The passage goes on to describe the vicious misdeeds of the tyrants. The wages of the hireling were being unjustly withheld. The widows and orphans were undergoing intemperate unmerited oppression. Strangers were denied their fundamental rights.

There are a few situations that get under the skin of God. While it is true no sin is above the other, we do find convincing language in the Bible that unambiguously demonstrates Gods' anger against those who would deal unrighteously with widows and orphans. God always fights for those who cannot defend themselves. I can only imagine the consequences of those who have slaughtered unborn children through abortion. Hell will have no mercy for the thousands of (un-repented) abortionists as well as the mothers and fathers who sacrificed their precious babies on the altars of self.

The fact is, as angry as God was with those children for their hideous sins against Him, as well as society at large, God was prudent to remember the covenant He made with their fathers. The Lord reminded the Israelites He was not going to change His mind about the promises He had made, even in spite of the open shamelessness they showed Him. The Lord goes on to remind Israel, because they are the sons of Jacob they are not consumed, *"For I am the LORD, I change not; therefore ye sons of Jacob are not consumed,"* in His righteous judgment.

I don't know about you, but if I were God I would have toasted those folks really well for their sins and oppression toward those innocent people. However, I am reminded of Romans 3:23, *"For all have sinned, and come short of the glory of God"*. Their sins are inexcusable as for God's judgment, but who are we to throw stones? The same mercy God showed those Israelites, He has ministered to you and me as well.

You may ask the relevant question, "but if God is God, why can't He just destroy those people and proceed to greener pastures?" Simple, God is constrained by His Word. The sovereignty of God is only restricted by His Word. God never strays from what He has declared in His Word. If He said it, He will do it.

For time's sake it would be impractical to go into detail regarding the sovereignty of God. Henceforth, in compliance with His own Word, God has made certain unconditional as well as conditional promises to His Children, the Israelites, and He can't just annihilate them as some would think He could. Despite Israel's long-term relationship with the false gods of this world, God has made certain promises that involve the preservation of Israel.

The passage in Malachi quickly points out the disgust God felt toward Israel in that for many years they had been unfaithful to Him. Our passage is clear; from the time of Israel's fathers they had been irresponsible in their commitment to righteousness. The Bible says in Malachi 3:7a, *"Even from the days of your fathers ye are gone away from Mine ordinances, and have not kept them..."* Israel didn't get into the shape we find them overnight. From Genesis to Malachi we observe the slow spiral descent into man's wickedness and evil ways.

There is a lesson for us to learn here. Wickedness is patient; it usually doesn't happen overnight. Wickedness always intensifies with time. Wickedness dulls the senses of those caught up in it. Wickedness is the devil's standard of living, just as Holiness is God's standard of living. Sin piled on sin piled on sin is soon the apparent manifestation of wickedness. Wickedness is always separated from the things of God. One cannot be wicked and be righteous according to that which is imputed to us as children of God.

If a person sins, it doesn't necessarily mean he is wicked, or that he is the child of Satan, but nevertheless, sin is NEVER excusable in God's eyes. Sin will always take from a person that which can never be completely restored.

Chapter 14: God Never Changes, People Do

Consider the sin of Adam. Look at what sin cost Adam and Eve in the Garden. I once heard someone explain sin and the devil like this, if you let the devil take the wheel he will take you somewhere you don't need to go, keep you longer than you want to stay, and cost you more than you are willing to pay.

It wasn't God who changed in this passage in Malachi; the children of Israel had changed. God was always right there pleading for them to come back and repent of their evil deeds. As we continue to read in verse 7, *"Return unto Me, and I will return unto you, saith the LORD of hosts"*. Our Lord here is pleading for them to come back and serve Him. Notice, we always have to return to God He is always there for us, but we have to cry out to Him. We are the ones who have to repent for forsaking Him. We are the ones who must confess our sins, not God.

Sadly we learn the children of Israel had been living in sin for so long they had no idea of the distance they had drifted in their relationship with God. After years and years of continual wickedness, Israel had no idea they had strayed away from the faith. Time had taken its toll. They were shameless in their own conceit. After all, God was quick and compassionate to point out their sin, loving enough to reach out, forgiving enough to ask them to come back into the fold. His children were so blind and deceived in their heart they asked God, *"Wherein shall we return?"*.

Sadly, we are as guilty as those Israelites when it comes to asking God about our own careless ways and backsliding. We can hear a great message at church and think to ourselves, "Wow, that preacher laid it on *them* folks." "Why, he smoked the church up real good today." "Did you see how old so and so was looking?" The real truth of the matter is that the Lord may have been trying to speak to you and me, instead of everyone else.

Most people find it easy to see the flaws in others, but we are often so callused with our own problems that the Word slides right off with out taking root. Friend, be warned: we never arrive. God is always moving. You and I should always be conscious of what is going on around us, even if it deals with sweeping up around our own back porch.

Time has a way of taking a toll on the circumstances around us. We become accustomed to things that at one time offended us. Then, we manage to look the other way. Sin never changes its effect, nor is the price ever discounted. There are no blue-light specials when it comes to righteousness. My friend, our actions and the actions of people around us are either right or wrong in the sight of God. There are no gray areas.

Have you let the enemy dull your senses? Do you find yourself compromising on issues which used to be so important? Let me ask you this, have you changed your mind, or has God changed His? Has the absolutely unacceptable become tolerable in your home, in your work, and with your friends? Have you changed your mind, or has God changed His?

We all suffer from memory loss at one time or another; however, we should never forget our convictions. Nor should we forget those things that were once wrong in our eyes. We should never be so narrow-minded we begin to be self-righteous, or as I like to say, suffer from a "Religious Spirit". Let us strive to serve God in every means possible, that is, as long as it lifts up Jesus and never draws attention to either us or any other person.

Times have changed so much. As a society we have compromised in so many ways. I remember when I was a boy; you never saw a dead person's body on the news. Such tragedy was only referred to and never focused photographically on. Today, we not only see the dead on the news, but I have actually seen people gunned down live before a news cameras.

Remember the Gulf War or, should I say, "The Hollywood War"? The media had news persons scattered all around in both allied and hostile territories. We saw the skies light up over Baghdad as it happened. We watched as guided missiles videotaped their path and point of destruction. Remember the elevator shaft? We all watched as a missile was guided right into it. We saw abandoned vehicles with bodies wasting away beside them. The poor hungry Iraqi troops were shown live as they surrendered. Yes, we saw it all. I saw, by means of the media, a real war fought in the comfort of my own home.

I remember the movie or documentary "Holocaust." I was very young and not allowed to watch it, but I remember sneaking, on the floor out of my bedroom and seeing just bits and pieces. I can't remember all I saw, but I was shocked at the things I did see. Twenty-five plus years later, many children wouldn't think twice nor bat an eye at the tragedies committed by the Nazis.

Twenty years ago in America, you would never have seen a half-naked man or woman standing in the bathroom advertising hygiene products, would you? Today, you can see anything you want on television. It seems there are no limits to what you can see or hear anymore. What was once

Chapter 14: God Never Changes, People Do

rated "R" is now simply PG. Years ago you never heard of Psychic phone lines and telephone sex. Only in the last decade has so much putrid filth been spewed out into our living rooms.

The other day I was in a room having lunch with some co-workers when I looked across a table to see a magazine with a picture of a woman's backside completely nude. I was shocked and could not believe what I was seeing. I was even more shocked to find out it was a women's magazine that could be purchased in any department store in town. I ask this question, what will we tolerate tomorrow if we let these things slide today? How far are we willing to go before we draw a line and say this is it?

Some people who seem to want to have their little sin and filth, merely improvise ways to get around or justify them. People are very quick to point out excuses as a way of dealing with such intolerable issues, after all it is a new century – Right? Wrong! Excuses must cease, and we must get back to God's Word.

We learned in Malachi God didn't try to smooth out their wickedness with excuses of their inability to live up to the law. He was clear about explaining their sins and offered His hand to those who would return unto Him. He reminded them he had not changed; He was going to be faithful concerning His promises. Sadly, the problem God encountered was getting them to admit to their sin.

The lesson to learn here in Malachi is that God doesn't change. Israel, in their pursuit of righteousness, had strayed far from what we know was true righteousness. We learn Israel would try to, and most often did, kill those prophets who would proclaim God's Word and point out their wicked ways. Much of their ridiculous laws were birthed out of their own efforts to justify what they once knew was evil in the eyes of the Lord. Did God change, or did His people?

As a Christian, God's unchanging ways excite me. One important fact concerning God's character is He is always the same. Even though the children of God were consumed in all sorts of wickedness, God remembered He was to respect the covenant made to the fathers of Israel. As much as God may have wanted to zap them from the face of the earth, He was committed to His Word.

Today we can take courage in God's unchanging ways, just as men and women have for many thousands of years. We must realize God will be faithful concerning every promise He has made to us in His Word. Whatever

God's Word states about an issue, we can bank on it as believers. If God has declared a promise in His Word, we are to be filled with anticipation of its coming to pass. No matter what the situation may be, or the circumstances surrounding us, we are to take joy in what God is about to perform.

My friend, just as God's judgment will never change for the sinner, we have the assurance that God's love and mercy will never change for the Saved. It is clear whatever side of the judgment one may stand on, we can be certain that God is the same yesterday, today, and tomorrow.

There is a beautiful scripture in the book of Numbers I take great comfort in. It is a great verse to dedicate to memory, because it demonstrates the integrity of God so well. We read in Numbers, 23:19 *"God is not a man, that He should lie; neither the son of man, that He should repent: hath He said, and shall He not do it? or hath He spoken, and shall He not make it good?"* What a wonderful example of God's commitment to what He has promised each person in Scripture. So much can be learned, and so many can be comforted by this verse.

People often get into situations where it is so easy to blame God when things go south. In years of ministry, I have come to learn many people enjoy "butting" against the Word headfirst. It is as though God's Word will bend for them in some way. Then, when they inflict great pain or tragedy on themselves or others, they shake their fist at God.

Now, I have had plenty of times in my life where I just poured it all out on the line before God. I have been in seasons of my life that I wasn't doing things just the way God wanted me to. It is easy to get self in the way. And in such times I can remember feeling so angry at God for my own mistakes. After all, God's immeasurable size offers a great target for people's gripes and complaints, but I learned a long time ago no matter what people throw at God, He is big enough to take it.

Have you ever noticed that those who seem to have a lackadaisical attitude toward God seem to put up the biggest fuss when they suffer a bad situation in their life? It is usually those who rarely, if ever, go to church who seem to complain and moan at God for not answering their prayer. I bet God gets so sick of hearing the whiny prayers of those who never mention his name or dart in church except on Christmas and Easter. Sadly the holidays are as close as many get to joining the church.

I once heard it said, "there are no atheists in foxholes." Remarkably, many have a way of finding their way back to God. Unfortunately, it is often "too

Chapter 14: God Never Changes, People Do

little, too late". While we may have to endure the continual nagging of the sinner and immature Christian, we that are willing to trust God at His Word can breathe softly when unwanted circumstances come our way.

Does God change when we take center stage in life's often, unpredictable arena? No. God remains committed to His Word, and may I add, committed to His children as well. We change. We are the ones who pull away from God. God is always faithful. He will never let us down. He will never abandon us because He is, once again, committed to His own Word. Consider the following Scripture and His ever-present integrity.

> *The Lord is not slack concerning His promise, as some men count slackness; but is longsuffering to us-ward, not willing that any should perish, but that all should come to repentance. (2 Peter 3:9)*

Let us look at Peter, a wonderful man of God, a great evangelist, yet so unpredictable in scripture. In some places in the Word, Peter's behavior reminds me of so many Christians today. God's children would do well to learn as much about Peter's life as they can. There is so much encouragement and strength to be drawn from this precious man of God.

Not only can Peter be known for his great evangelistic efforts on the Day of Pentecost which saw thousands saved, but his continual failures can give us encouragement as well. Peter's life and ministry is one to be revered by many, but we all can see ourselves in his shoes at certain times. We can learn a great lesson on God's faithfulness by looking at how Jesus handled Peter's doubting faith when he walked on water.

> *And when the disciples saw Him walking on the sea, they were troubled, saying, It is a spirit; and they cried out for fear. But straightway Jesus spake unto them, saying, Be of good cheer; it is I; be not afraid. And Peter answered Him and said, Lord, if it be Thou, bid me come unto Thee on the water. And He said, Come. And when Peter was come down out of the ship, He walked on the water, to go to Jesus. But when he saw the wind boisterous, he was afraid; and beginning to sink, he cried, saying, Lord, save me. And immediately Jesus stretched forth His hand, and caught him, and said unto him, O thou of little faith, wherefore didst thou doubt? And when they were come into the ship, the wind ceased. Then they that were in the ship came and worshipped Him, saying, Of a truth Thou art the Son of God. (Matthew 14:26-33)*

In verse 27, we see Jesus manifesting His unchanging love for His disciples. Just when the men on board were stricken in fear, for they feared the presence of a ghost, Jesus reached out to calm their fears. It is unique to notice how scared and superstitious these grown men were when they saw the supernatural. I can't criticize them too much. Many of us may have acted the same, or worse. The important fact is - Jesus discerned their fear and quickly bade them to be of good cheer and not to be afraid. What simple love Jesus demonstrated here in this passage.

Friend, Jesus is saying the same thing today. If you are scared and/or worried, be of good cheer and be not afraid. After all, was there ever a time when Jesus allowed any of His disciples to remain afraid? Did he ever let any of His disciples down? No. Jesus always calms our storms and brings a flood of peace when we simply allow him to. Jesus' love for us has not changed a bit since the days He walked with his disciples on earth. He is just as committed to resolving our fears and anxieties as He was 2000 years ago.

There may be circumstances in your life that are flooding in like a river, and you just can't seem to get above water. Perhaps you are scared and your back is to the wall, and no matter which way you turn, there is no escape. Jesus is faithful to see you through these situations. You must be willing to cry out and have complete faith in our Lord. Just as Jesus stretched forth His hand to Peter that day on the sea, He is stretching forth His hand to save you from drowning in your own fears.

Another interesting point to observe in this passage is Jesus' willingness to allow Peter to exercise his faith. Imagine having the faith to walk on water, as Peter exemplified in this passage. Often I hear sermons on Peter's attempt to walk to his Master on the water. The sermons seem to focus on poor Peter's sudden fear and lack of persevering faith. However, Peter did walk on the water, which is more than I can say for those on the boat, myself, those critical ministers, and everyone else I know. A person's faith pleases God.

> *But without faith it is impossible to please Him: for he that cometh to God must believe that He is, and that He is a rewarder of them that diligently seek Him. (Hebrews 11:6)*

From cover to cover, the Bible urges us to exercise our faith. There is no place in scripture that teaches us to suppress our faith nor deny ourselves from maturing in faith. Jesus was urging Peter to exercise his faith. We can call it what we want, or explain it in different contexts if we wish, but when Peter asked the Lord if he could come unto Him, Jesus replied "...*Come.* And

Chapter 14: God Never Changes, People Do

when Peter was come down out of the ship, he walked on the water, to go to Jesus."

I could not imagine my feet stepping on water like Peter's did. That had to be some sight to see. What a testimony of God's power! First, the whole boat load of men saw Jesus walking on the water. Then, they got to see their friend Peter walking on water as well. I bet there are people today who would say to themselves, "If I would have seen those miracles, I could never doubt God's power." Wrong! Where were most of the disciples when Jesus was crucified? They were nowhere to be found!

I can just imagine it in my mind right now. Seconds are passing, Peter is having the experience of a lifetime as he pursues his Master. Then, all of a sudden he looks away from his Master, and there he sees a boisterous wind. What happens next is so typical of all of us when we take our eyes off Jesus. The Bible says Peter was afraid and began to sink. Notice here the passage didn't say he sunk, it says *"...and beginning to sink..."*

Beloved, there is absolutely no stability apart from Jesus. There is no assurance when we look in another direction for our refuge. Ultimately, we will sink in any situation if we do not have our eyes fixed on our Redeemer. The Lord is our only refuge in life's stormy seas. We cannot afford to take our eyes off Him, even for a second. Our enemy is present to snare us anyway he can, and you can bet he will use any and every situation to have us take our eyes off our Lord.

Peter was exercising his faith and encountered no problems until he saw the boisterous wind. He took his eyes off Jesus and gave doubt an opportunity to work. Beloved, doubt is an enemy of your faith and is ALWAYS a hindrance to the work of God. I Repeat, doubt is an enemy of your faith and is always a hindrance to the work of God.

There is not a doubt in my mind Peter had to make a decision at this point on what to do. Peter had several options. First, he could have called on the others to help him. Secondly, he could have tried to swim for it. It is no doubt Peter, being a fisherman, knew how to swim well. Lastly, he could look to Jesus and call on Him.

After weighing his options, He cried out to Jesus saying "Save me". Yes, Peter realized the circumstance was too big for him to overcome because he feared for his life and needed saving. Peter chose to be saved by Jesus Christ instead of looking to the others in the boat. We too must look to Jesus, and not others around us, to draw faith from. Remember - parents, siblings, children, family, friends, co-workers, pastors, etc., will let you down. Put your faith in the One who will never leave you nor forsake you (Hebrews 13:5b).

Did Jesus change His mind and allow Peter to sink? No. Did Jesus turn His back on Peter when he needed Him most? No. Who changed in this passage? Was it God in His unfailing love and protection? Or was it Peter in his sudden lack of faith in the midst of surrounding circumstances? It was Peter. God never changes; we do. Peter was quick to realize his only solution to his crisis. The Bible says, *"and beginning to sink, he cried, saying, Lord, save me. And immediately Jesus stretched forth His hand, and caught him, and said unto him, O thou of little faith, wherefore didst thou doubt?"*

Notice how quickly Jesus exposed Peter's problem in the passage. Jesus had no sooner caught him by the hand when He confronted Peter with his reason for sinking in the sea. The fact could be argued over what caused the wind to stir about the time it did. Some would argue it was the devil, some say it was the Lord testing Peter's faith.

To make my point, the reason is irrelevant. The fact is you are going to have circumstances arise, situations which will often seem inescapable. Those crises can be brought on by a host of reasons, as well as people. The question is, how will you respond? The origin of the problem is of no concern when getting through it is the issue at hand. Once you're through a crisis, then you can consider the reason, the culprit, and etc. Peter didn't try to figure out from where the wind and waves were coming. He wasn't concerned whether the Lord or Satan was testing anything, he merely was acting upon demand... sink or be saved!

What will you do when everything around you is about to literally bury you? Is there a problem that lies ahead in your life? The way to deal with it is to go right through it; stand firm in your faith and march right through the situation that is confronting you. What about a situation that is piling up and you know you will eventually have to sort through it? Are you scared of what you may find? Are you scared of some kind of humiliation? Are you afraid of losing a friend or the closeness of a family member? Maybe you are afraid to face your fears. Perhaps your fears have you hiding from others.

Friend, step out of your crisis and reach for God's hand. You might say to yourself, "But I'm safe as long as I remain in my boat." No, you are only prolonging the inevitable. You see, eventually, if the winds had not ceased,

Chapter 14: God Never Changes, People Do

the boat Peter was in would have capsized. Don't let circumstances crash your faith. Remember God is with you all the way. If you delay, the seas of life will drown you - then where will you be?

The Lord wants you to take Him by the hand and forget what is going on around you. Don't try to face your problem alone. Peter made the right choice after he doubted. He cried out for Jesus, and the Lord was there for him at that critical time in his life. God didn't do any favors for Peter; He is not a respecter of persons (Acts 10:34). What the Lord offered Peter that day He offers us today - His hand, help, healing, and heart!

Friend, it may seem safe where you are, but it isn't. You must realize you cannot manage your situation alone. You need God's unchanging hand. Yes, Jesus was there in person to help Peter, but He is there for you as well. The Bible says, *"Let your conversation be without covetousness; and be content with such things as ye have: for He hath said, I will never leave thee, nor forsake thee. So that we may boldly say, The Lord is my helper, and I will not fear what man shall do unto me (Hebrews 13:5-6)."* Let the Lord help you today. He will never leave you nor forsake you.

You may be saying, "That was then and this is now, how can I be sure God will be there for me?" Remember, God hasn't changed; He is there for you as well. Peter was not more important to God than you are. God loves each person equally. Let's look at what Peter said concerning one of the characteristics of God, *"Then Peter opened his mouth, and said, Of a truth I perceive that God is no respecter of persons: (Acts 10:34)"*

If your ship is sinking in life's storms, remember that only when Peter and Jesus were in the ship did the wind cease. Just because you have taken a hold onto the hand of God doesn't mean your situations are going to dissolve. It may take time to reach a place of total refuge. No one knows how far the ship was from Peter when he began to sink. What we do know is that the winds ceased after they both were in the boat.

In conclusion we must accept the fact that Peter, while holding on to the hand of Jesus, walked through the raging waters that were caused by the boisterous winds. Did Jesus take Peter out of his circumstances? No. He simply took him by the hand and led him through the circumstances to the ship. On their way to the ship, the wind blew and the waves smashed against the boat tossing it around like a toy.

Today, there are many who teach that all of life's problems will be over when you accept Christ as Savior. Wrong. Others teach if you are exercising your faith, crises will not come. Wrong again. Remember, Jesus had all power, yet He Himself walked with Peter through the boisterous winds and raging seas, choosing not to calm the storms until they were both in the boat. "*And when they were come into the ship, the wind ceased. Then they that were in the ship came and worshipped Him, saying, Of a truth Thou art the Son of God*".

Even Jesus had to suffer afflictions while on this earth. Those who were around Him suffered as well. The night He was to be openly betrayed by Judas He prayed in the garden that His cup be removed. However, He went on to say, *"not My will, but Thine be done."* Afflictions are as much a part of life as brushing your teeth. It is how we handle life's problems that separate us from others.

Is it right for us to assume whenever we encounter affliction we are to look outside ourselves for the source of the problems? No. Often we do have ourselves to blame. We are not perfect. Many times we make poor decisions, often having long-term effects; in short, we reap what we sow.

It would be safe for any of us to always look within for the problem before looking or blaming others. Let's ask the Holy Spirit for guidance to search our hearts to see if there be found anything unworthy. King David said it like this, *"Search me, O God, and know my heart: try me, and know my thoughts: And see if there be any wicked way in me, and lead me in the way everlasting (Psalms 139:23-24)."*

Beloved, stay focused on Jesus through all things. Remember to trust that God is one who is constant, not changing all the time as the weather. The focus here is for each of us to apply our faith in the assurance God is the same today as He was yesterday and as He will be tomorrow. When we are truly confident in this truth, we can have tremendous faith.

Prayer:

Lord, help me to trust You more and more each day I live. Help me to realize that truly You will never leave nor forsake me. Help me to claim scriptural promises when the enemy comes against me and my faith. Lord, help me to grow in strength each day I live, that I would someday be able to stand tall in my faith. More than that, I want to always keep my eyes on You, Lord. Wherever my faith takes me, I want to give all glory to You. Help my walk with You to be a testimony to others of Your unchanging love and protection. Amen.

15 | The Spirit Of Fear

Fear is an enemy of the child of God. If you want to see a beautiful work of God get stalled, just watch fear literally stifle the life out of it. What makes fear so powerful is the way it works in the life of a believer. Fear works from deep inside the soul of man, surfacing only in desperate situations. You see, most of the time we Christians can keep fear suppressed, however, fear is always accessible when the child of God is exercising his or her faith.

The truth is - fear, doubt, and unbelief are kind of like the opposite poles of faith. You will never see a successful Christian who is making an impact for our Lord Jesus Christ, gripped and oppressed with fear. Christians who are living a life of constant doubt and unbelief will never deliver the Gospel, nor live a faithful lifestyle the way they were intended. Fear is a dominant characteristic. Fear does not want to play second base in a Christian's life. Remember that fear seeks to control the life of the believer.

> *For God hath not given us the spirit of fear; but of power, and of love, and of a sound mind. Be not thou therefore ashamed of the testimony of our Lord, nor of me His prisoner: but be thou partaker of the afflictions of the gospel according to the power of God; Who hath saved us, and called us with an holy calling, not according to our works, but according to His own purpose and grace, which was given us in Christ Jesus before the world began. (2 Timothy 1:7-9)*

Let us be honest with ourselves. Each one of us knows what it is like to be afraid. Fear isn't something we encountered the first day we got saved. Fear didn't swell up the first time we felt led by God to do something. We have

Chapter 15: The Spirit Of Fear

been battling various fears all our lives. We battled it as a child and we have had to confront it as an adult. We didn't have to wait to learn what fear was, it made its presence known very early in our lives. I think it would be safe to assume fear has taught us well.

People have been battling fear from the first time their parents turned their back on them in the crib. Many dealt with it going to school the first day. We dealt with it once we got to class and hesitated to speak out in fear of being made fun of. Later, it was fear of rejection, men failing to ask that special girl out because of the ever-present possibility of getting turned down. Then, perhaps, it was moving out for the first time, or leaving home to attend college. Yes, fears have always been there, and notice how fear always wants to keep you from accomplishing something great in your life.

I found a wonderful web-site that is published in conjunction with the US Department of Navy. The web-site deals with briefs, how to prepare, deliver, and finish one. Of course one of the issues they have to address is the most common, fear. What is interesting is they go on to identify the other top nine and give their advice on how to overcome the first one. Here are the top ten fears ranked from greatest to least: Speaking before a group, heights, insects and bugs, financial problems, deep water, sickness, death, flying, loneliness, and dogs.

Once the slides presented the fears, they gave practical advice on how to resolve the first and most common fear – "Public Speaking". According to the slides, we first practice what we are going to say. Second, remember to take deep breaths. Third, be yourself. Fourth, and final, you have to believe in what you are saying. One person wrote "The brain starts working the moment you are born, and never stops until you stand up to speak in public" – Anonymous.

One of my worst fears is a storm; particularly storms which produce high wind such as hurricanes and tornadic weather. I can handle the thunder and everything else, but the wind continues to frighten me until this day. I have managed to get much better with dealing with this fear.

One very special guest we have to put up with when living on the upper Gulf Coast is hurricanes. I have seen a lot of them and obviously survived. As a result of living in this area, each year I always make sure I am well stocked on needed materials to weather one if I have to. It beats last minute preparations all to pieces; you will have to trust me on that one.

Most fears are a result of some past experience in your life – mine is no different. As a child I remember sitting out on my grandmother's porch listening to her tell old stories about tornadoes. I would sit there with great hope of the day I could see one. In fact, I was very passionate about tornadoes. I would go out during thunderstorms and look into the skies just hoping to get a glance of one.

My anticipated chance soon came. One summer's day, my family and I were sitting in our living room during a severe thunderstorm. I don't remember why, but for some reason I was looking out the window. Suddenly, there it was, just like I had seen in the movies, the very tail of a tornado being sucked up into the cold dark clouds. I was so excited all I could do was yell, "I saw one, I saw one, I saw a tornado being lifted into the clouds." Well, no one believed a word I said. It wasn't over a minute until the news broke into the programming and warned of a tornado being spotted in the Wilcox area. Right where I saw it! I was so happy – it could well have been Christmas for me.

But the ultimate introduction to tornadoes was yet to come in my life. My life long quest was answered one school morning a little before nine o'clock. I was in my first period class when the weather started getting dark outside the room. My schoolroom was very typical of the architecture of classrooms during the early eighties, brick over block with windows in the back from waist to ceiling.

As I peered through the windows, I could see the night-lights were lit across the campus. As I sat there in the well-lit classroom it was obvious the yard was getting darker by the moment. In only moments it could have well been night and no one would have known the difference. Actually, I don't think till this day I have ever seen it that dark in the light of mid-morning.

Then what I kind of expected happened. The teacher told us if we heard a bell start ringing, we were to come immediately to the front of the classroom and lay our heads – she never finished her comment. Windows began to shatter. Students ran for their lives to the front of the classrooms. Unfortunately I never made it more than a few steps from my desk when I was forced on the floor by debris and wind. I remember putting a jacket over my head and two other guys joined me under there as well. What seemed like forever was over in seconds.

Moments later, the wind subsided and I realized I was still alive. What used to be a block wall in front of me was now ripped apart and I could see

Chapter 15: The Spirit Of Fear

outside. My body was covered from head to toe with glass and cement. Scratched from one end to the other, clothes ripped and snagged, soaked to my feet from water, bleeding from all the scratches, I realized my dream had finally come true, a dream I wish I never had. It goes without much thought to say, from that day forward I have been somewhat afraid of storms – with good reason. From that day on, I would have great respect for storms.

There are fears that are good. In fact, fear of hurricanes and predictable weather is somewhat good. Why? It causes us to be prepared for circumstances that could arise. If you have ever lived on the Gulf Coast during the hurricane season, you know people always run to prepare before the storm hits. Grocery stores are packed as people buy non-perishable items to survive during the frequent and sometimes lengthy power outages.

Unfortunately, fear often hinders people from ever starting anything that is not guaranteed to work, or is not completely safe. It is fear that keeps me from starting the so-called hobby (tempting God) of skydiving. This fear is not a good one to have though. Life is full of chances, and often to get ahead we must take them. Nothing is for certain. To be successful in many things, there has to be a chance taken – consider those who invest in risky stocks and funds and become millionaires over a short time.

Some wrestle with fear of rejection. They never start anything in their life because they are always consumed with what everyone is thinking. The fear someone will criticize and even laugh paralyzes many. Fear of rejection is very common; it is like a cancer eating at an individual. Fear of rejection will leave one very depressed and lonely in the world we live in. Sometimes, we have to just bite the bullet and move on without concerning ourselves with the thoughts of others.

Two Basic Fears

There are two fears I like to refer to as the Fear that Protects and the Fear that Paralyzes. The fear that protects is that part of constant awareness of the things around us that would do harm, both in the physical and the spiritual. For example, in the physical, we should never live in fear someone is going to break in on us, but we should always take safety measures such as locking the doors. We understand the physical laws of science to know we cannot safely make it around a sharp curve driving excessive speeds. We know to always let a radiator cool before adding water.

These fears simply protect us from circumstances around us. It is a very safe fear to have and to give into at all times. Just think of all those people who determine to stay in the path of a category four hurricane, or children who deliberately fly kites in and around power lines and are harmed or killed. Fear that protects does just that, it protects the individual from avoidable accidents.

On the spiritual side of the fear that protects, we should always be discerning of the things around us, concerned where we are, moreover, concerned about those around us. We should never put ourselves in compromising situations with the world. It is true we should not be in fear of the world, nor of sin, because 1 John 4:4 reminds us, *"Ye are of God, little children, and have overcome them: because greater is He that is in you, than he that is in the world."* Consider Matthew 10:28 *"And fear not them which kill the body, but are not able to kill the soul: but rather fear Him which is able to destroy both soul and body in hell."* Rev. 19:5 *"And a voice came out of the throne, saying, Praise our God, all ye His servants, and ye that fear Him, both small and great."*

The second fear is that of paralysis, better understood as the fear that paralyzes us from moving ahead in our life. In like manner, this fear can affect us both in the physical as well the spiritual. This fear is always harmful. It is never good in any way. This fear will always keep us down and keep us from achieving things in the natural and in the spiritual. Very candidly put, this is the "Spirit of Fear." It is a gripping, paralyzing force that attacks at the smallest hint of advancement, achievement, and success.

There is that opportunity to move to a new city to advance in your career, but you are gripped with the "What ifs." God is calling you to teach Sunday School – "What about..." You want to take a course in – "But, but." You feel like you should stand and testify – "What will people..." Get the point? It limits. It holds back. It hinders. It simply paralyzes the body and the soul of man from making any advances in the right direction.

God is constantly calling men and women to do His work, but with each call there is a host of fears that arise. These fears manifest themselves in all sorts of ways, but the end result is the same – FAILURE. The shame of it is we let Satan talk us out of all kinds of opportunities to not only use the faith we possess, but the chance to build our faith as well. Remember, if God has called you, God has or is equipping you!

Chapter 15: The Spirit Of Fear

Perhaps there is a fear you need to overcome today. In the last two years think of how many times you have wanted to do something for a great cause and you let fear hold you back. Be honest. I know it hurts, but each of us know of these unfortunate situations, both in the natural and in the spiritual. Well, my friend it is time and high time we took up arms against the monster of fear. We don't have room for fear in our lives, especially those of us who have been saved by the Grace of God.

Not to meander off the subject, but have you ever noticed how fear never affects the gambler. He can lose all kinds of money, and he is right back at it again and again, he never gives up on trying and failing to pursue his greed. However, we Christians can get a black-eye from something and will retreat every time there is the slightest opportunity of confrontation in what we once failed. Isn't that a sad testimony of God's people?

Let's move deeper into understanding fear. Let's consider Satan's purpose for our fear. Satan is a master at using our fears. Notice I said OUR fears. Not our parents', our preacher's, our children's, but our own. By using our fears against us, he will keep us from being an effective Christian or a happy person.

He uses the "Spirit of Fear" to make our lives miserable. He can make us so afraid of losing our jobs, our wealth, and our home. We can become so paranoid we fail to enjoy all God has blessed us with. Consider the misers who are blessed with an enormous amount of wealth, but are afraid of losing it all, so they literally starve themselves of great opportunities such as family and vacation, even denying themselves a proper diet and medication when sick.

I once read about a lady who died in 1916 named Hetty Green, "The Witch of Wall Street." She was called America's greatest miser. When she died in 1916, she left behind an estate valued at $100 million. But she was so miserly she ate cold oatmeal in order to save the expense of heating the water. When her son had a severe leg injury, she took so long trying to find a free clinic to treat him, his leg had to be amputated because of advanced infection.

Through fear Satan makes us ineffective. Ineffective because we fail to share our faith with others because we are so bombarded with these useless and often cowardly thoughts: What will they think of me? They probably won't listen to me anyway! What if I turn them off? What if I mess up? All these statements and questions are common fears Satan uses to make us ineffective witnesses.

Many times Christians will not involve themselves because of fear. The enemy allies with our fears and begins to tell us what we can't do for the cause of Christ. This anti-serving spirit has wrecked the modern church. The fear of involvement has weakened the outreach of the New Testament church into our communities, creating a host of problems such as divorce, crime, and immorality of all kinds.

Some would beg to differ with this conclusion. However, we must realize God commanded us to go out into all the world. He volunteered us for the job. We have a responsibility to be a witness to all men and women. We are each a member of one body, having a particular function as a living body for Christ. When many fail to do their part in the Great Commission, the body is weakened all over. Many times this trend can be traced to fear, rather than rebellion to God's Word.

Let's consider how Satan uses this fear to keep us from involvement. The word "can't" comes to mind as I consider this part of fear. I can't teach a Sunday School class. I can't help in the nursery. I could never be a pastor, minister, or missionary. Beloved, who told you that you can't? Seriously, who told you such a thing? In Romans 8: 37, the Word reminds us that YES, we can. Consider the verse, *"Nay, in all these things we are more than conquerors through Him that loved us."*

As we move deeper into understanding fear, we will now focus on Satan's method for using fear against us. Remember, fear is an instrument of control. Men have used fear to control homes, communities, religion, and countries since the beginning of time. It is a sure thing when applied properly, but God wants us delivered form its grip today.

Satan will use four ways to immobilize the Christian with fear. First, he uses our past sins. Listen, God has forgiven you and cast your sins into the sea of forgetfulness. We have all sinned and come short, my friend. Each of us has sinned miserably in the sight of God. As a child of God, we must put off that cloak of condemnation that the devil wraps us with and move out full force for the Gospel's sake. There is a lost and dying world out there waiting for you to bring them hope. In fact sometimes you can use those past sins to help people grow. You see, you have potential no matter how you have lived your life in the past.

Chapter 15: The Spirit Of Fear

Secondly, Satan uses the possibilities of the future. Don't worry about tomorrow. Let tomorrow take care of itself. Focus on today and what you can do for the cause of Christ. Focus on what God is doing today in your life, your job, your career, your church, and your family.

> *Therefore take no thought, saying, What shall we eat? or, What shall we drink? or, Wherewithal shall we be clothed? (For after all these things do the Gentiles seek:) for your heavenly Father knoweth that ye have need of all these things. But seek ye first the kingdom of God, and His righteousness; and all these things shall be added unto you. Take therefore no thought for the morrow: for the morrow shall take thought for the things of itself. Sufficient unto the day is the evil thereof. (Matthew 6: 32-34)*

Thirdly, Satan uses the potential of failure. Be honest. Who hasn't failed at some point in their life? Every great invention and discovery was marred by failure right after failure, until one day a break came. Consider the outcome if Thomas Edison would have decided to give up on the light bulb after his first experiment failed.

I am sure you have failed before, and you still do from time to time. But may I remind you, if you are following the will of God, friend, you cannot fail. You are destined to victory when you have the Lord on your side. Yes, the enemy will be there to remind you of past failures and to try and scare you about potential ones. Remember what the Word says, "*What shall we then say to these things? If God be for us, who can be against us?*" (Romans 8:31)

Fourthly, Satan uses the certainty of criticism. We will be criticized by family, by church, and of course, the world. It will happen. However, you should never let fear of criticism slow you down in the least bit. It is inevitable, so why even bother worrying over it and letting the inevitable ruin your life? No man is above criticism. Criticism is as sure as the rising of the sun.

I like to think of it this way, Jesus Christ the Son of God walked this world having never sinned, He healed and touched lives you and I will never be able to number. Yet, angry religious leaders followed Him from the time He opened His mouth till the day He died on Calvary. He was criticized, ostracized, but He continued to fulfill not His own will, but His Father's who sent Him.

The worst thing you can do in this life is to try to please everyone. You will be a basket case in a very short time. While we should do our best not to offend, we certainly will offend, especially when it comes to being a Christian in this society. Let's consider what the Word has to say about this point.

> *Woe unto you, when all men shall speak well of you! for so did their fathers to the false prophets. But I say unto you which hear, Love your enemies, do good to them which hate you, Bless them that curse you, and pray for them which despitefully use you. (Luke 6:26-28)*

There are ways that God gives us the ability to rise above these fears. Consider the passage we started this chapter with:

> *For God hath not given us the spirit of fear; but of power, and of love, and of a sound mind. 8Be not thou therefore ashamed of the testimony of our Lord, nor of me His prisoner: but be thou partaker of the afflictions of the gospel according to the power of God; 9Who hath saved us, and called us with an holy calling, not according to our works, but according to His own purpose and grace, which was given us in Christ Jesus before the world began... (2 Tim 1: 7-9)*

Satan is the master at using our fears to stop us, to bind us, and to rob us. However, through His Word, we see God has given us three gifts, or weapons, to overcome fear with. With this Scripture we have the ordinance to fight against all fears Satan would strike us with. Here are the gifts as they appear in our passage.

First, we have the gift of power. Through Christ Jesus I can do anything God wants me to do! *"I can do all things through Christ which strengtheneth me (Philippians 4:13)."* That means anything God wants me to do, I can do it. Through this wonderful power I have the power to be saved, *"But as many as received Him, to them gave He power to become the sons of God, even to them that believe on His name: (John 1:12)"*

I have the power to be a witness for Him, *"But ye shall receive power, after that the Holy Ghost is come upon you: and ye shall be witnesses unto Me both in Jerusalem, and in all Judea, and in Samaria, and unto the uttermost part of the earth (Acts 1:8)."* I have the power to be joyful in all circumstances, *"Now the God of hope fill you with all joy and peace in believing, that ye may abound in hope, through the power of the Holy Ghost (Romans 15:13)."*

Chapter 15: The Spirit Of Fear

I have the power to be a strong, steadfast witness of the Gospel, *"Now to Him that is of power to stablish you according to my gospel (Romans 16:25)."* And last but not least, I have the power to endure trials, *"And He said unto me, My grace is sufficient for thee: for my strength is made perfect in weakness. Most gladly therefore will I rather glory in my infirmities, that the power of Christ may rest upon me (2 Corinthians 12:9)."*

Now, let us return back to our main passage and see what our next gift to overcoming fear is. We see after having the gift of power, the Bible tells us that we have love. That's right, love. I remember a sermon where the minister outlined this passage in dealing with fear. I thought to myself, what does love have to do with fear, and then it began to make sense to me.

Let's consider this scripture, *"There is no fear in love; but perfect love casteth out fear: because fear hath torment. He that feareth is not made perfect in love (1 John 4:18)."*

Friend, have we had anything positive to say about fear? Fear torments the mind. Love always heals and nurtures the body, soul, and spirit. Here is how this works: we have love for God and love for others. We know we are the children of God. We know He is going to watch over us in all situations.

What we as Christians must realize is that God will take care of His own. When we truly began to comprehend this promise, our fears will soon subside as our faith in God emerges out of the darkness of fear. That is right. With God all things are possible.

> *And we know that all things work together for good to them that love God, to them who are the called according to His purpose. (Romans 8:28)*

When we are in God's will, we are in His purpose. Things will have no other option but to conform to the will of God. It doesn't matter how things look, feel, or seem. If God has ordained it, it will work. Love of God is synonymous with trust in God. You can't love something without trusting in it as well. Remember, *"He that feareth is not made perfect in love."*

Secondly, while on the point of love, we must consider not only love for God, but love for others as well. Love conquers fear. You say, "I don't understand." Love overcomes fear for the good of others. How many times have you done something spontaneous that could have been dangerous, but all you thought of was the safety or welfare of a loved one, friend, co-worker, or even stranger?

Consider rescue workers, firemen, policemen, military personnel and ambulance drivers. They often have to put themselves in harm's way, but never do they back down because of fear. I have heard countless stories of how a family member rose to the occasion to save a loved one in a dangerous situation, never considering their own life being at risk. They acted in a swift manifestation of love.

I served in a volunteer fire department for years. I constantly had myself in harm's way, but I never gave it a thought until after the fact, if I thought about it at all. What would possess a person to do such a ridiculous thing? Simple love for my fellow man – that is all. Millions of people put their own lives on the line everyday for the safety of others.

Thirdly, in our passage we read of the gift of a sound mind. So far we have looked at the gift of power and the gift of love. Now we conclude with a close look at the mind. I think one of the most wonderful things God does for us when we come into the fold is that He heals our mind as well as our spirit and body.

Some people are fearful of tomorrow and what it may bring. We don't ever have to worry about who is in control of our lives. The Word assures us the Lord is looking over us and all our affairs. Sinners are always concerning themselves with the things of the World, the things in the natural, but the Word says:

> *And be not conformed to this world: but be ye transformed by the renewing of your mind, that ye may prove what is that good, and acceptable, and perfect, will of God. (Romans 12:2)*

Consider this verse as well:

> *If then God so clothe the grass, which is to day in the field, and to morrow is cast into the oven; how much more will He clothe you, O ye of little faith? (Luke 12:28)*

Remember, part of living is dying. We have nothing to fear but fear itself. Did you know our biggest victory over the devil comes at our death? That is right. After death we are eternally healed, spared of all the problems of this world and secure from all temptation. Consider the Word on this subject:

> *We are confident, I say, and willing rather to be absent from the body, and to be present with the Lord. (2 Corinthians 5:8)*

We could go on and apply this to every other fear we may have.

Chapter 15: The Spirit Of Fear

Beloved, we at last fight fear with the mind. We use the power of God, the love of God, and now the mind. You see, when we consider the Word and all its wisdom, we find ourselves bubbling over in faith. The Word teaches us faith comes by hearing and hearing by the Word of God. Once we have positioned ourselves against fear, using power and love, our intellectual man kicks in and relay's wisdom and knowledge to our spirit, causing us to swell up with overcoming faith that delivers victory over all fear.

In conclusion, let us be mindful of how the "Spirit of Fear" can rob us of enjoying a life filled with love, joy, peace, longsuffering, gentleness, goodness, faith, meekness, and temperance. We must be determined to look fear in the face and choose faith instead.

Every day we will have opportunities to apply faith over fear. Will we have the self-determination to say yes to faith and no to the "Spirit of Fear?" Conquering fear is a matter of total dependence in God, the One we can trust and love.

Prayer:

Lord, help me to rise above the fears that have robbed me in the past, fears that have held me back from living according to Your will, fears that have literally paralyzed me from being the servant You have called me to be. Help me to overcome my fears with the power of Your Word, Your love, and with the sound mind You have given me. Give me the courage to stand against all forces that would seek to destroy me from exercising my faith. In Jesus' name, Amen.

16 | Faith Fosters Fortune

Webster's Dictionary defines "fortune" several different ways. I define fortune as having all you need and having obtained all you want-- all you want out of life, out of people, out of your church, out of your children etc, etc, etc... Fortune is tangible for the child of God. Fortune is relative to each person. As beauty is in the eye of the beholder, so is fortune to the one who has found peace and contentment in all things, no matter how others perceive it.

Beloved, fortune is very relative. Many people will believe and trust God for things others could purchase out of their wallet. Today, millions of Christians living in famine stricken nations prayed and believed God for a meal. God honored their prayer just as one in the States may have prayed they would have the finances to treat a special guest to an exquisite meal. They both equally trusted the Lord to supply their needs, and for the exquisite meal, perhaps, their wants.

Somewhere in the world, Christians united and trusted the Lord to provide a much-needed rain to harvest a crop that was vital for survival. At the same time, someone was believing God for a clear smooth sea to try out their new yacht. God is omnipresent, processing and answering the prayers of millions, while honoring the simple faith of each that made a request.

As you can clearly see, we all apply our faith in God to obtain a vast array of wants and needs. I need a new pair of dress shoes to match my new suit. I believe God will give me the finances to buy inexpensive shoes to complete my outfit so I can land that job for which I am interviewing. Another person

Chapter 16: Faith Fosters Fortune

believes God for a pair of shoes so they can walk on the rough stones making up the ten mile journey to town. Same faith and need, just in different parts of God's created world.

Does God judge between the faith of the rich or poor? I don't think so. Will He honor the faith to provide for a need over a want? I don't think so either. God is big enough to reach out to all peoples, no matter their geographic location or social standing. His love for His children holds no boundaries. The faith of any child of God is just as real to the Lord as another child of God's, no matter where they live. God equally feels the love and trust of all that would make Him Lord.

My friend, millions are trusting in God for all sorts of things right this very moment. God is speaking to millions this very second. God is leading millions of people in the paths of righteousness, not only through Scripture, but through the voice of His Spirit as well. One man doesn't hold the attention of God. There isn't one person who can discern the voice of God from all others. You don't have to be tuned into a special channel and hear from a minister at a designated time to receive a miracle from God. God is not limited by one person or a group of individuals, rather, He is free to move in the lives of any and all that would trust and obey.

Man places the limitations on what God can and cannot do in their lives. Man erects the gate-valves which control God's bounty that flow in the lives of His children. To be honest, there are very few who have not placed limitations on what God can do, few who can earnestly look toward heaven and pray without restraining their faith. Remember, God has never put a cap on what you could ask for or trust Him in.

When Peter asked if he could get out of the ship and walk on water, Jesus immediately allowed Peter to exercise his faith. Peter did a wonderful job walking on water until he got his eyes off Jesus and placed them on the circumstance around him. Peter's mistake is a classic example of the unfortunate mess we find ourselves in everyday. We pray and believe. At the moment God starts to do the miraculous, we quickly focus on our circumstance instead of victoriously conquering our fears.

Beloved, we will all trust God for many different things as our lives go on. Some will only trust Him for the necessities of life while others will trust Him for all their wants, as well as their needs; God will honor both requests just the same. If we apply our faith, God will do according to His Word. Unfortunately, most will draw a figurative line in their faith and never cross over it. They will trust up to the imaginary line and never go beyond. In many cases, influential people, religious sects or denominations have determined the line for them. You can be sure of one thing; OUR faith will honor those lines of limitation, and OUR faith will never compete to cross over them.

Fortune is relative. Fortune is relative to the believer and what they choose to believe for. We will determine when and what we can believe God for based on the faith we have. Faith will be the vehicle to obtain our fortune from God. Only you and I will decide what that fortune might be. Remember, for each person there is a different idea of what fortune is, as well as a limitation of how much of it they can have. God will never lead us to put a cap on what we can trust Him for. The word will encourage us to apply faith and move into the promised lands of fortune.

Fortune has to be sought after. For everything for which we are trusting God, we most likely have a preconceived idea of how God is going to supply it. Sadly, these preconceived ideas often limit God, as detailed in another chapter of this book. For example, we want to purchase a wide-screen high definition television in March. We don't want to use a credit card and we know we can't have enough money saved up in time. What are our options? Lord, what can we believe you for?

Well perhaps, first of all, do we really need the television? Perhaps if we had some extra money in our pockets we should pay off the bills that are accumulating at 22% interest. But wait, the answer is here; let's believe God for a really big tax return this year. Perhaps we know our tax return is going to be $3200.00. We will simply use the money the Lord got us on our tax return – praise the Lord!

What we have really witnessed is limitations placed on a request and poor stewardship to boot. First of all, the Lord didn't "get" anything for us, we simply overpaid the government money we could have used during the year, or we qualified for some tax incentive or discount.

Next, we determined the source for the miracle God was providing for us. I guess, on the positive side, we saved the Lord some leg work, but perhaps God was going to lead us in a different way to come up with the money, plus have the $3200 tax refund to pay off some debt.

Perhaps what God had in mind was to open up an opportunity to make some extra money working a few hours a week on the side. Granted, He could have led someone to just give you the money. God is not limited if we

Chapter 16: Faith Fosters Fortune

don't give Him limitations. While it is true we had to seek after a means of obtaining the $2800 for the new television, God never even considered the price tag. He went straight for the source of capital to purchase that item you prayed for.

Now, while the point of limiting God has been dealt with redundantly, God does use practical means of blessing His children. God never wants us to limit His hand; however, God wants us to grow in wisdom and knowledge. Take for example King David, I believe David was made wealthy because of his faith in God, and therefore God's unlimited bounty flowed into David's life. David knew how to praise and worship the Lord and grab hold of God's heart.

David knew how to pick up an instrument and worship the Lord with all his heart, making joyful songs and divine music. David's music was so anointed it healed and drove evil spirits away. David's fortune came from a God Who rewarded him because he knew how to praise and worship, making the Lord feel loved and honored. David had a relationship with Jehovah like none other – he knew His heart and ministered to the Lord, as we see recorded in so much scripture.

Solomon, on the other hand, was given great riches by his father David, but God increased his riches by giving him the most priceless fortune building gift of all, wisdom. Solomon took wisdom and intrigued the whole world with his fortune. A wise man will always be a fortunate man indeed. Solomon knew how to make the right decisions at the right time, which yielded short-term and long-term growth. God was still the author of Solomon's fortune, and no matter how much sin Solomon fell into, God was still the giver of his wisdom.

Today God gives us wisdom as well. He gives us wisdom to properly seek after fortune on our own, using the gifts He has given us. Let's consider a person who wants to make $150,000 a year. There are four ways he can achieve this goal, he can earn it, he can inherit it, someone can give it to him in 52 divided installments a year over the rest of his working career, or last, but not least, God can put a hundred dollar bill in the mouths of fish and he can spend the year fishing everyday – except on Sunday, of course.

Most likely, but not for certain, the means that God would use would be to give us the courage and strength to endure four to seven years of college earning a professional degree in a lucrative field of study. During the schooling, God would increase our knowledge and expand our faith as we believed Him for good grades and the means of meeting all our needs. For God to work in this matter, we may ask the question, have we limited God in any way? No. Will life continue to offer countless opportunities to trust in Him and have unwavering faith? Yes.

Suppose you have inherited four thousand acres of beautiful land in Arizona's desert. Let's say you have determined to grow Douglas Firs to harvest for Christmas trees. Now for the reality check. You don't have the funds to put up a screened area to block the sun's unmerciful heat and devastating rays, nor can you afford a vast irrigation system for your water supply. Your only other means of success in the Christmas tree business is Faith. Don't hold your breath. You know the sun's heat will scorch the needles off the tree in three hours of heat, and the average rain fall is a fraction of what you will need to supply the roots with proper nourishment, not including the lack of proper nutrition in the soil.

The faithful prayer of the righteous will prevail. God will honor faith, and fortune may be right around the corner. But, what if God is speaking to your heart and leading you to plant a cactus farm instead? I'm not saying God has to make sense, but wouldn't that make a lot more sense? Beloved, it is no accident that God, who planted the earth to start with, chose not to put cactus in the rain forest and bamboo in the desert. The idea of your ingenious business is akin to raising starfish in freshwater ponds. While you have the right to believe God for anything, asking Him to redesign the plant and animal kingdom for a business venture is pushing the point to say the least.

Seek the Lord and His guidance for fortune. Fortune has to be sought after; it doesn't just happen; there are practical paths to follow; and God is there to usher us in those paths. We must put our trust in His wisdom, not in ourselves. Fighting against wisdom to assert we are applying faith is foolish and detrimental to our relationship with God. In all we do we have to seek first the will of God in our life. We apply our faith toward the will and wisdom of God in our life, and fortune will follow.

As for the four thousand acres and what to do with the land, maybe you could raise rattlesnakes and sell the venom to make serum, sell the meat to food distributors, and sell the hides for boots, belts and hat bands. All these ideas are practical, and God can open heaven and pour out a fortune of money in sales.

Chapter 16: Faith Fosters Fortune

Fortune has to be sought after. God gives us the ability to go to the right places and meet the right people. God is for us. He is never against us, but we have to align ourselves with wisdom and seek in the right places and faces that which we count as fortune. For one to sit and pray without ceasing for God to grant them a 52" HDTV in a country that doesn't have electricity for two hundred miles and short-wave radio is the best form of entertainment, is frightening. Yet, we believe for some of the same things comparatively. Practically speaking, consider what it will take to purchase, deliver, power, and maintain the set. To add insult to injury, we are going to need satellite to pipe the signal in to such a remote area.

Fortune has to be sought after with prayer and great wisdom. We have to allow God to speak to us in making full application of our faith. Whatever we call fortune in our lives, it will require works added to our faith. We may have to aggressively pursue a plan to achieve fortune. Through wisdom, God can assist us in mapping out a clear route to success in whatever we are pursuing.

The formula for fortune is faith plus works. When we put faith in action, or shall we say works, we will achieve results. God isn't pleased with spiritual and physical slothfulness. There is a certain common sense that goes along with faith. For example, if you want a job, get up and look for one. If you want to be a doctor, spend the next seven years passing medical exams in college. If you want to work at Wal-Mart, go to the manager and apply for a job. If you want more time to read the Bible, stop watching TV and start reading instead. To lose weight, eat less and increase physical activity. To play the piano, get lessons and start practicing.

Fortune has a cost; life isn't free, nor is God's plan for man. While we teach salvation is free, which it is, afterwards God calls us to His service. He gives us life eternal and then calls us to spread the same Gospel that led us to repentance to the rest of the world. The Lord wants us to share Christ with our friends, families, neighbors, strangers, and even co-workers.

For God to lead us to the fortune we desire, it may require us to move away from friends, family, and loved ones. For all fortune there is a price; nothing is free. If we didn't have to pay the fare, someone did. If you enjoy a wonderful Christian family, you can rest assured someone had to reach each family member with the message "Jesus saves". The message was free, but to deliver it didn't come cheap. Someone had to be bold enough to proclaim the truth to your family member at the cost of possibly losing a friend forever. They had to make time for the visit and most likely used their vehicle and gas to make the contact, all of which had a cost.

If your home is part of your fortune, you or someone had to pay for it. If your spouse is part of your fortune, you have had to love and nurture that relationship. Most likely, you have had to bite your tongue instead of spewing poisonous words of hurt to your loved one. You may have had to put up with behaviors and incidents when it would have been easier to walk out the door. The everyday battle to stay in physical, mental, and spiritual shape so you can enjoy life, as well as your spouse, has had its cost. Through it all, God builds in us the faith we need to acquire our fortune.

True fortune requires us to share and empower others. As God leads people to fortune in life, He gives them a desire to share their fortune with others, especially loved ones. In the Bible there are many instances of fathers leaving their children great gifts, including land, jewelry, and spoken blessings. Generations were often blessed with the fortune of one man, such as Abraham.

Through the lives of everyday individuals acquiring their fortune, God has countless opportunities to teach the hard lessons of life, saving others from having to make the same mistakes. In fact, one of the reasons for this book is to share what I have learned about faith as I have obtained so much fortune in my life. I have been down the hard roads. I have come to the drop-offs of life and felt defeated. I have had my faith tested and made foolish decisions when I should have either listened to God and/or waited on Him.

One of the most exciting things I do now is speaking blessings to as many people as I can. I seek after opportunities to impart some wisdom God has taught me. I love people so much I honestly make an effort to coach them away from the pitfalls of life and the disappointments to which poor decisions will lead them.

I remember the commercial Coke used to run when I was a little boy, the song "I'd like to buy the World a Coke" Oh – if I could only share my faith with all, if I could only walk the aisles of salvation for everyone who is lost. I wish I could go into the hospitals and clean them out with the gift of healing and/or prayer of faith. All I can do is share the fortune God has given me, and determine to always share His Grace, love, mercy, and simple truths to all who would lend an ear.

Chapter 16: Faith Fosters Fortune

Fortune gives birth to fortune. Like the old saying, "the rich get richer and poor get poorer", it is not hard to see the truth there. I seek occasions to bless people as much as I can. I pray God would send the right people to me that need assistance in some way. I pray for good discernment in giving to others. I pray God sends me the right individual or couple that needs a blessing sown into their lives. Perhaps they need that little boost of support that comes from someone's fortune.

I take great pride and comfort in understanding the laws of sowing and reaping. As I impart some area of my fortune to others, I know God will impart a blessing in return. I can't help that God has established certain truths, and one is give and it shall be given back. I can't help that as I give sacrificially God opens heaven wider and returns more fortune to me. Beloved, that is the wonderful God we serve.

I think I know why God loves a cheerful giver. A cheerful giver gets excited about an opportunity to bless and can't help but to be gleeful at the fact that whatever he just gave will come back multiplied so that he can give more of his fortune the next time around. When you really understand fortune, faith comes easier and easier. My friend, faith truly fosters fortune.

I remember some of the hardest times when I was just starting out on my own. I was a zealous preacher with good intentions, but often making some foolish mistakes. I loved the Lord and was filled with imperfection from head to toe. I felt so unworthy of God's blessings. It seemed that God kind of stretched me out to the threshold of breaking before He would provide at times.

I remember that work was good, but it barely paid the bills. Preaching on weekends earned me a little and occasionally God would lead someone to put in a really big offering. Those days were great, but they were hard times. I trusted and studied God's Word and stood faithfully on His promises. I knew that no matter how things looked, God could not lie.

During the tough times and search for the right paths, I met my wife, who I actually had known all my life. The thought of marrying her never entered my mind, even when we were going out. It's a long story – but to the natural mind it was an impossibility. In time friendship grew into love, and the rest, well the story is always the same.

My wife and I did a lot of talking when we dated. We both wanted a traditional home and lots of children. My wife wanted to be a stay at home mother. I wanted to be a go to work dad. Unfortunately, I had a job I loved, but it didn't pay the bills once "Junior" came along. My wife had worked right up to the day she went into labor, and both of us knew that the day labor started was the day her job, which she loved, was over.

A few years before we had our son, God had spoken to a person who had achieved some fortune in his life. God promoted him to a wonderful job which gave him the opportunity to sow into the Kingdom of God. As he sowed, God blessed him more and more, and he was led to sow into our ministry. The Lord used him to practically match my income and provide for our family when we needed it the most. Trust me; our son Christopher didn't come cheap, just like all children.

Faith fostered fortune, and fortune reached out and shared with this minister. God had pointed a servant in the direction of fertile ground in which to sow. I didn't realize what God was doing, but my friend did. God had been teaching him valuable lessons regarding faith and the sowing of seed. As for my wife and me, we were delighted to be blessed with the gifts that flowed into our lives. I didn't really understand all that was going on at the time. My friend insisted God was blessing us and raising us up for something big.

He was convinced our ministry was an investment. I received his kind words and often struggled to believe what God had led him to do. I knew one thing above anything else, my friend was a true man of God and I felt God's presence on his life the first time I met him many, many years before. Separated by hundreds of miles we kept in touch. I had my world and he lived in his, but our friendship grew.

A strange thing had happened to me, because for years I served the Lord and never really had a big paying job with all the benefits like many of my friends. I worked jobs that offered an opportunity to be a part of people's lives, especially those who really needed influencing in a positive and Christian way. I always prayed about my work, I always wanted more money, yet for some strange reason I knew I was where I was supposed to be. I had made a decision to never work for the money, because I would never spend eight hours a day doing something I hated.

As I trusted God, I was told over and over by some that knew me that the jobs I had were stepping stones to something bigger. I found it hard to always believe what others were telling me, and even what I really felt in my heart was the truth. At the time it was hard to believe, especially when the bank account was empty, but I persevered and continued to believe God in

Chapter 16: Faith Fosters Fortune

all His Word despite what seemed to be the obvious – poverty. Darlene and I prayed for an increase and a good stable job that would meet our increasing financial needs. At the same time, my friend still sowed into our lives, and others would bless us as we continued to minister the Word.

One day an opportunity came for us to go into business when an attempt to get a raise at my job had failed. I loved what I was doing and wanted to stay in the same field for the rest of my life. I was dedicated to my work and God blessed me abundantly with promotions, yet to raise a family in this economy, demanded so much. And even worse, our commitment to be a single income home challenged us, but we never wavered in the promises of God's word.

All the prayers begin to pay off as the new company opened for us. The business instantly grew and I made more money the first month than I had ever made on a job in that same amount of time. The second month God increased it a little more. In three months I now made as much as most people I knew. At a time Darlene and I needed the finances, God came through. What was miraculous was that my friend called me up one day and regretfully said God had directed him to start giving to another person or persons. I was filled with joy when I heard those words. I could now tell him to take his money and fulfill God's will in another person's life.

Fortune shares and faith fosters fortune. God spoke to me and then called me to do the same thing as my friend had obeyed God and done for us and others. I began to put into motion the wisdom of others and the wisdom God had imparted to me. I realized growth was dependent on duplication of myself. I knew I had to work and perhaps, as you learn in network marketing, I needed to have more Melvins working every day to increase revenue.

God opened up the means to start an agency with my business, and my first employee brought over several clients from a business she worked for that had closed. Again, God sent the right person at the right time and faith fostered more fortune. The cycle of duplication had evolved into a wonderful agency that grew tremendously well in the face of cuts, a poor economy, and rumors of bad news.

Today, I continue to minister to anyone who will listen. I have committed to investing into the Kingdom of God every time I get an opportunity. I have passed and continue to pass on as much wisdom about faith and the wonders of God as I can. My friend we hold the keys to the Kingdom of heaven. We have a direct line to the bounty of heaven and my aspiration in life is to share with many people the good, the bad, and the ugly aspects of faith, fallacy, and fraud.

The fact is I had to go down many roads to get where I am now. The Lord is still the same; the battles are all the same as they were. God is still building faith in my heart, and I trust Him for more ways to enrich the lives of others. I have many more years of hard work ahead. I have so much to do and so much to give. I never thought I would know what fortune was at such an early age. I never thought I would see a time I would try and give all that I could away only to have God pouring it back into my life multiplied.

Beloved, give, give, and give. Give your time, your talent, and your tithe. Remember the only thing you can take to heaven is what you have given away. Don't let the enemy short change you in understanding faith. Understanding faith is as much understanding what it isn't as understanding what it is. Knowing who you are in the Kingdom of God is as vital as praying for who you are going to be. Remember the wisdom and lessons I have attempted to show you in this book. I pray that they will uplift your heart and increase your faith.

Faith fosters fortune, but remember, fortune is what you make it. Fortune isn't limited to financial wealth. Fortune is what you possess. Fortune isn't just material property. Fortune cannot be burned in a fire. Real fortune can't be stolen or taken away.

Do you have fortune? What has Faith produced in your life and the lives of those around you? Fortune is to be shared. If what you perceive as fortune cannot be shared then it is not fortune, perhaps merely riches. A life of Faith will produce fortune every time.

Beloved, we have journeyed many miles down the highway of faith. I pray that you have been encouraged. I pray you have received Strength from God's Word and the testimony I have shared. Remember real Faith cannot be received by our five senses; however, you will ALWAYS sense Faith when it is alive.

17 | The Plan Of Salvation

Statistically, most people agree there is an after-life. Have you ever thought about where you will spend eternity after you die? As you well know, sooner or later everyone will suffer death in some manner. Your death may be quick and tragic, or perhaps it will come at the end of a long and fruitful life. Life is very uncertain, and the moment you die may come at any time.

By now, you most likely know friends, family or neighbors who were unfortunately killed in an automobile accident. Others may have suffered a devastating stroke or heart attack and had no time to say goodbye to loved ones. We all know tragedy can happen so quickly, many people have no time to even speak a word before that fatal moment.

After death there is one of two bodies you will inherit. One of the bodies requires a decision on this side of death; and the other body is given by default to those who postponed a decision or simply ignored the opportunity to decide for various reasons.

If you have not taken the time before, you will now be given an opportunity to take a few moments to make an important decision. Depending on what decision you make, your body could be supernaturally transformed into a perfect body that cannot suffer death or destruction. Then if you were to die, you would never again suffer pain and heart-ache. You will be immortal in every sense of your imagination. There will never be tears of sadness, and all calamities will be over for eternity. Your days will be spent in pure joy and breathless splendor.

Chapter 17: The Plan Of Salvation

Preparation for this body requires a person to make a decision on earth at some point in their life. The decision is simple and FREE. All you have to do is simply ask Jesus, the Son of God, to save you and believe by faith He has granted you eternal life by your request only. There is no fee or effort involved in accepting what is called Salvation.

For those who never took a moment of time in their life to request salvation, they will inherit eternal damnation and suffering that will never cease. The Bible describes a place of eternal torment where there is constant weeping and gnashing of teeth, yet no deliverance will ever come from literal flames of fire that will burn the flesh of man yet never consume him. Friend, there is no death and no escaping the eternal torment. Some would say this is cruel and absolutely ruthless punishment; perhaps it is.

Keep in mind, all a person has to do is repent of their sins and make a quick simple decision to trust Christ as their Savior, a decision that takes moments but lasts a lifetime spent on earth and all eternity. What is sad is that a person could have made this decision while driving down the road, eating a sandwich on a lunch break, waiting in a teller line and so on. Someone could have taken a moment before going to sleep or perhaps while taking an early morning shower.

When you think of all the opportunities, there is really no excuse. In fact, if you haven't taken an opportunity to make your decision, now would be an opportune time. Today is your day. This is the day you can receive Salvation. Today is the day you can be sure you will be eternally saved. After you make a decision to trust Christ you will never have to be unsure of your life after death. I can promise you today you can be sure, and I will further explain why you need Salvation and answer a few common questions.

One may ask the relevant question, "Why do I need to be saved?" In the beginning when God made man, He put them (Adam and Eve) both in a Garden and told them to multiply, and they were without sin before God. However, there was one command God gave them in the Garden.

> *And the LORD God commanded the man, saying, Of every tree of the garden thou mayest freely eat: But of the tree of the knowledge of good and evil, thou shalt not eat of it: for in the day that thou eatest thereof thou shalt surely die. (Genesis 2:16-17)*

It wasn't long before both Adam and Eve had eaten of the forbidden tree, and because of God's Word man had to die. Man had to die naturally and spiritually. The natural death would come in time, but the spiritual death was immediate. Because of the sin of one couple, Adam and Eve, God cursed them and drove them out of the Garden and out of His presence. From that time until now, every child born has been born living outside of the presence of God. Because of the nature of sin, and the curse of God on Adam that day, sin has forever passed down through the blood of every person born thereafter. This action has separated each person from God, because a Righteous and Holy God cannot look upon sin. Therefore, man fell out of fellowship with God.

> *Wherefore, as by one man sin entered into the world, and death by sin; and so death passed upon all men, for that all have sinned. (Romans 5:12)*

Friend, that's only the beginning of the story. You see, God loved man, He loved man so much, according to the Bible; he visited with Adam and Eve in the cool of the day. Can you imagine the Lord wanting to walk with you each day as well? Did you know he wants to walk with you as He did then? In fact he wants to put your past behind Him and not only walk with you, but live inside of you. The problem is, because you are a sinner you have been sentenced to death and, therefore, you are separated from God. Did you know everyone has sinned and everyone has been sentenced to death?

> *For all have sinned, and come short of the glory of God. (Romans 3:23)*

Of all the people who have lived on the face of this earth there has never been a person naturally born outside of sin. There has never been but One who could stand before God declaring himself righteous and without sin. No matter how good you are, you are not good enough before a righteous God. The Bible declares, *"There is none righteous, no, not one (Romans 3:10)."* *"But we are all as an unclean thing, and all our righteousness are as filthy rag.(Isaiah 64:6)."* So you see, friend, it's nothing personal against you and what you might have done; it's a matter of our sinful condition in the presence of a Holy God.

Yes, friend, there is no hope for mankind trying to save himself, for his fate is death just as sure as there is a God. Some believe if they live right and do good deeds they will eventually make it to heaven, but good deeds will not save you. The Bible says, *"For by grace are ye saved through faith; and that not of yourselves: it is the gift of God: Not of works, lest any man should boast (Ephesians 2:8-9)."* You see, there are plenty of people who are good folks and live a very productive, charitable life; but they, too, are sinners in need of a Redeemer.

Chapter 17: The Plan Of Salvation

Of course there is one way to be sure you can go to heaven. There is one way you can be acquitted from the sentence against you. There is One who can save you if you will put your trust in Him. That person is Jesus Christ. Jesus says, "*I am the Way, the Truth, and the Life: no man cometh unto the Father, but by Me (John 14:6).*" Friend, there is a price to pay for being a sinner. Sin has a cost. The cost is the death and separation of mankind from God forever. "*For the wages of sin is death (Romans 6:23).*" But today God has a special gift for you because He goes on to say in that verse "*but the gift of God is eternal life through Jesus Christ our Lord.*"

> *For God so loved the world, that He gave His only begotten Son, that whosoever believeth in Him should not perish, but have everlasting life. For God sent not His Son into the world to condemn the world; but that the world through Him might be saved. He that believeth on Him is not condemned: but He that believeth not is condemned already, because He hath not believed in the name of the only begotten Son of God. (John 3:16-18)*

> *But these are written, that ye might believe that Jesus is the Christ, the Son of God; and that believing ye might have life through His name. (John 20:31)*

My friend, you can be forgiven of all of your past and start all over again. All the wrong you have ever done can be wiped clean.

> *Come now, and let us reason together, saith the LORD: though your sins be as scarlet, they shall be as white as snow; though they be red like crimson, they shall be as wool. (Isaiah 1:18)*

Isn't that great news today?

> *Come unto me, all ye that labour and are heavy laden, and I will give you rest. (Matthew 11:28)*

Aren't you tired of running? I know you can use some rest. How would you like real peace?

> *And the peace of God, which passeth all understanding, shall keep your hearts and minds through Christ Jesus. (Philippians 4:7)*

Today, you must die for your sins. You must die to that old nature and let God resurrect your life. What you need to do is trust in the Lord Jesus Christ for your Salvation so you may be born again.

> *Marvel not that I said unto thee, Ye must be born again. (John 3:7)*

Jesus answered and said unto him, Verily, verily, I say unto thee, Except a man be born again, he cannot see the kingdom of God. (John 3:3)

You see, when you accept Christ as your Savior, you become a new person.

Therefore if any man be in Christ, he is a new creature: old things are passed away; behold, all things are become new. (2 Corinthians 5:17)

Jesus has paid your debt. God sent His only Son to this earth to live and die and be a sacrifice for your sins and mine. In order for God to give life back to man, a life had to be required. You see, someone had to love you and me enough to give their life in order for us to live.

But God commendeth His love toward us, in that, while we were yet sinners, Christ died for us. (Romans 5:8)

He not only died for us, but He took on our sins so we could be forgiven by God.

Who His own self bare our sins in His own body on the tree, that we, being dead to sins, should live unto righteousness: by Whose stripes ye were healed. (1 Peter 2:24)

There was a man that once asked the same question you may be asking yourself right now.

And brought them out, and said, Sirs, what must I do to be saved? And they said, Believe on the Lord Jesus Christ, and thou shalt be saved, and thy house. (Acts 16:30-31)

The Bible says, "*For he saith, I have heard thee in a time accepted, and in the day of salvation have I succoured thee: behold, now is the accepted time; behold, now is the day of salvation (2 Corinthians 6:2).*"

Are you ready to believe Jesus Christ is the Son of God and that He died for your sins?

Behold, I stand at the door, and knock: if any man hear My voice, and open the door, I will come in to him, and will sup with him, and he with Me. (Revelations 3:20)

If you are ready to repent of your sins and ask Jesus Christ to come in your heart and save you today, I want you to pray and believe this prayer right now.

Sinners Prayer:

Chapter 17: The Plan Of Salvation

Lord, I am a sinner, and I repent of all my sins. I believe Jesus Christ died for my sins. I accept by faith that His blood has cleansed me of all my sins. I receive Salvation by Grace alone, through Faith. Lord, help me to be Christ-like in all I do from here on. Help me to grow in wisdom and knowledge from this day forward. Help me understand Your Word and help me to let my light shine before all men. I ask all these things in Jesus' name, Amen.

My friend, welcome to the family of God. At this moment rest assured you are saved and justified before God. You can now enter in before God and have full fellowship with Him. In fact, you are not the same person you were a while ago. You see, now you have received the Holy Spirit. He has taken up residence in your heart. Yes, you have a part of God living in you right now. And if you will submit to God, the Holy Spirit will lead you in all truth.

If you accepted Jesus Christ as your Savior, I would like to hear from you. If you would, write me and share how God changed your life. If this book has inspired you through its message of faith and commitment to the spreading of the Gospel, I would like to hear from you as well.

Web Address: www.melvinbarnett.com

About The Author

Melvin Barnett has been ministering the Word of God since 1986. Today, the author enjoys life as a husband, father, and pastor. Through the years he has served in ministry under many titles. From working as a Chaplain in a substance abuse facility to serving as the Executive Producer of Christian television programs, he has been blessed to minister to a vast range of needs from people with various social backgrounds.

Melvin began ministering the Gospel at the age of seventeen. He has a Shepherd's heart and distinctly enjoys teaching the Bible, evangelism, and one-on-one encouragement through life coaching.

Contact information can be found at www.melvinbarnett.com

www.ingramcontent.com/pod-product-compliance
Lightning Source LLC
Chambersburg PA
CBHW061647040426
42446CB00010B/1629